REBEL WITHOUT A CLUE

TALES OF
AN IMPERFECT MAN
IN AN IMPERFECT WORLD

CHARLES LEVINSOHN

INTRODUCTION

THE DAYS JUST KEEP ROLLING by. I don't know where they go. My head hits the pillow every night. I lie on my side and stare at the light creeping through my window until I drift off into sleep and dream. I wake up thinking that I dreamed something profound, but I never remember what it was. It escapes my consciousness as secretly as it entered. The next morning, I watch my feet hit the floor as the new day begins and think to myself, *I'm still here.* This happens over and over again. Decades have flown by just like this.

I wrote my first essay fifteen years ago, entitled "Time Waits for No One." I stole that title from a Rolling Stones song. They stole it from someone else. It's not exactly an original sentiment. As an aspiring author, I put my personal stamp on this universal theme and managed to get my inconsequential thoughts published in some equally inconsequential periodicals. Now it's time to revisit this subject from my present and more weathered perch. From the cheap seats, I watch the fourth quarter of life unfolding with the added knowledge of what came before.

My writing has met the same fate that has befallen the creative endeavors of many aspiring artists. Musicians, writers, painters, and poets have approached the doors of recognition only to fall short of admission. As the saying goes, "Many are called, but few are chosen." The entry point for validation is sufficiently narrow to discourage many from carrying on with their dreams. Time passes, and enthusiasm slowly recedes into the background. The majority of fallen artists move on to more attainable goals such as family, money, and social status.

I have persevered because I find satisfaction in crafting sentences evoking both humor and depth. If my words ring the bell of truth, then I have suc-ceeded. Whatever praise I might receive from my limited readership is enough to sustain me. I always welcome constructive criticism because even I wish to improve myself, as hard as that is to imagine!

As time goes by, I am aware that familiar names are disappearing from the ranks of the living. This is amplified by news flashes of Hollywood celebri-ties who have passed away. We assume a kinship with them from watching their movies, but we never really knew them. In many ways, they were ordinary people just like us, but for better or worse, fame and fortune thrust their private lives into the public eye. In the end, their personal histories recede into the sands of time, but their cinematic performances live on forever. The In Memoriam segment of the Academy Awards recognizes the recent passing of movie stars, and oddly, it is my favorite part of the show.

But what about the rest of us whose accomplishments are not so noteworthy? Are we just grains of sand blown into oblivion? Like Leonardo DiCaprio's final line in *The Gangs of New York*, "For the rest of time, it would be like no one ever knew we was ever here."

Regular people maintain their immortality through the legacy of their children and their children's children. Their names are spoken in reverence from one generation to the next, as the chain of succession remains unbroken. But I have no children. My artistic contributions as a writer will not be remembered unless I hit a home run in the ninth inning. The odds of that happening are not very good—I'm simply running out of time. If only I had started writing earlier! My secret mantra whispers in my ear, *Never a break, never a break...*

The reality is that my name will rarely be spoken. This may be hard to believe, but I am really not trying to be morbid. The truth is that I will have been here for at least seventy years and counting. For seven decades, I have been flying blind, often landing in situations that I never could've foreseen. I went with the flow and took on many challenges, excelling in some and failing miserably in others. I have had a subtle impact on numerous people over these decades, although many of them might not remember me. At least my name will appear on a headstone (I have a reservation).

It seems that the older you get, the more you think about stuff like this. In James Fenimore Cooper's classic novel, Chingachgook was *The Last of the Mohicans*. He wore a belt of woven beads representing the record of his life. As it turns out, I might be the *Last of the Levinsohns*. This is the record of my life.

CHAPTER ONE

LONG LIVE THE VOLTAIRES

I ALWAYS TRY TO MAKE MY way down to the beach on beautiful Indian summer days. The breeze feels nice against my skin, and I can smell the salty air as I breathe in deeply. This is where I find my center—embracing my Oneness with the Universe, even if only for an hour or two. I've been doing this for years, and there is some positive cumulative effect, although I can't exactly quantify it. I just know that it exists.

If I close my eyes as the waves are gently washing up against the shore, I can be transported to another time and place. I find myself at the Colony Surf Club circa 1963. I am on the beach at the Jersey Shore with all my buddies—teenage Jewish boys lying on towels, drenched in suntan oil, listening to a transistor radio. "Sherry" by the Four Seasons is playing, followed by "The Lion Sleeps

Tonight," "It's My Party," and "Sealed with a Kiss." What a time to be alive! We watch the girls walking by in front of us. For some reason, we are fascinated by the ones who live in different towns than our own. They are mysterious and alluring in their newfound maturing bodies. They feel our hungry young eyes on them as they pose, attempting to act unaware. We know that they know that we know. The dance has begun. The seeds have been planted for a lifetime of girl watching, the universal pastime of guys around the world and across the sands of time.

Just closing my eyes on a quiet beach leads to visions of things that actually happened and also things that did not. The line between the two gets blurry. Sometimes I fall into this recurring dream in which I'm driving over a high bridge that spans a large body of water, and my destination is unknown. I get off on an exit that immediately feels wrong. It leads me way out into the country to places I've never been, and I impulsively turn down some remote road where I never see another car. I am lost, but everything is beautiful and peaceful, so I just keep going. Turning around is not an option since I could never find my way back. I don't know what any of this means. Maybe it's about crossing over into the Hereafter. It's hard to say.

As a kid, I had a recurring dream that was less peaceful. I remember watching Tarzan movies starring Johnny Weissmuller on *Million Dollar Movie*. I'd end up having nightmares of being chased through the jungle by hungry tribes of cannibals. I'm lucky I wasn't permanently damaged by those visions.

When I was ten, I actually saw Johnny Weissmuller at the Monte Carlo Pool in Asbury Park, which was advertised as "The World's Largest Saltwater Pool." He gave me his autograph on the back of a baseball card. I got the courage to go off the high dive that day for the first time. That was a good day.

Back on the beach, the seagulls are making a racket as they dive after small fish that have risen to the surface. I slowly open my eyes after having drifted off once again. The sunny day has changed into one featuring an overcast and threatening sky. The ocean is steel gray with a visible riptide sweeping to the right. Looking around, I find I'm the only one left on the beach. I feel like the last person on Earth following a nuclear holocaust. Suddenly, right in front of me, two young women emerge from the surf. Two more survivors of the blast! They stumble to the shoreline, fortunate that the powerful current didn't carry them away. Maybe they're eighteen or nineteen years old. They gather themselves and turn to face the ocean. They're wearing European string bikinis, completely exposing their shapely posteriors. Am I still dreaming?

They're ten yards in front of me, directly in my line of vision. I have to look—after all, I'm not going to get up and move my chair. It's like I'm back at the Colony Surf Club, only it's almost sixty years later! Nobody revokes your girl watcher's license when you hit seventy. It's a lifetime position, kind of like being a Supreme Court Justice.

As it turns out, the Colony was eventually demolished along with its neighboring club, The West End Casino. They were replaced with condominiums, and both beach clubs are now barely remembered. But before they vanished from the face of the Earth, my teenage band, The Voltaires, secured a seasonal gig playing on the Colony's summer stage. The Voltaires—how did we come up with that one? Named after a French philosopher and adorned in uniforms of maroon velour shirts, black pants, and Beatle boots, we made quite a splash. Of course, we weren't yet old enough to drive, so our parents had to take us to the gigs, hauling our equipment in the backs of their station wagons. We had to rent the microphones from Scott's Music Store on Main Street in Asbury Park and had enough money left over to purchase mother-of-pearl business cards. Our names and instruments were printed in each corner: Jeff - drums, Chuck - lead guitar, Dick - rhythm guitar, Mike - saxophone. Jeff is my oldest friend, and we've remained close all these years. In his famous shoe box of souvenirs, a few of those faded cards still exist along with our earliest playlists. Maybe not as valuable as Beatles memorabilia, but priceless, nevertheless.

In 1963, Jeff's father, Seymour, drove a few of us up to New York to see Murray the K's *Golden Gasser of Stars* at the Brooklyn Fox Theatre. Murray Kaufman was a famous DJ and entrepreneur who promoted and hosted a series of shows that attracted such high-profile acts as The Miracles, Chubby Checker, Jackie Wilson, and The Isley Brothers. He hired a first-class orchestra to back them up. One group after another performed their greatest hits and then rushed off the stage as the next group came on. The energy in the Brooklyn Fox Theatre built to a crescendo with each successive act. We were just kids, sitting there in a state of awe. As far as other kids' dads went, Seymour was a cool guy. He wore Beatle boots and a leather jacket and happily drove his son and his friends to New York to see Murray the K! I credit Seymour Sussman with instilling in us a lifelong love of music.

Around 1965, there was an abundance of talented musicians performing at the Jersey Shore. I saw a local band featuring a guitarist whom I had heard about. Billy Ryan was nailing guitar solos on hits like "Johnny B. Goode," "Louie Louie," and "Hang on Sloopy." I ended up taking some lessons from this guy. I would never come close to being as good as him, and I knew it. He taught me the cool intro to the Beatles song, "I Feel Fine." Just learning that riff was an inflection point for me. After that, all things seemed possible.

I didn't hear Bruce Springsteen play until a couple of years later. I snuck into the now-forgotten Pandemonium club out on Highway 35. He was in a band called Child, and they were covering the Led Zeppelin song, "Dazed and Confused." His guitar work was electrifying, and his charisma filled the room. Who knew this skinny kid from Freehold would someday become a global superstar and be inducted into the Rock and Roll Hall of Fame?

As for The Voltaires, we made our bones covering top forty hits like "Twist and Shout," "House of the Rising Sun," and "Love Potion Number Nine" (with yours truly on vocals). We would mix in classic surfing instrumentals like "Pipeline," "Walk Don't Run," and "Wipeout." My favorite was "Sleepwalk" by Santo and Johnny. I played lead guitar with maximum reverb as the kids gratefully slow danced, pressed against each other's bodies on those hot summer nights. Whenever I hear "Sleepwalk," I'm transported back to that age of innocence.

Mike, the sax player, introduced us to a jazzy tune called "Comin' Home Baby" that was made famous by the Velvet Fog himself, Mel Tormé. It was an odd addition to our playlist, which normally featured such lame-brained hits as "Wooley

Bully" and "Land of a Thousand Dances." It was in the key of B flat, which was a fucked-up key to play guitar chords to, but Mike nailed his solo, and his sax never sounded better. Unfortunately, he was off-key on every other song. Was he playing all those songs in B flat? It was a mystery that we could never solve. We may have been called The Voltaires, but we were not deep thinkers.

Ultimately summer ended, and there was always something melancholy about that. In those days it meant having to go back to school. As you get older, it takes on a different significance—probably related to the cliché of being closer to the end than the beginning.

After our breakout gig at the beach club was over, the band broke up due to "creative differences." We returned to high school as juniors, preoccupied with more pressing matters, such as girls, homework, and sports. My maroon velour shirt was retired to the back of my closet, never to be worn again.

It's a shame there are no videos or recordings of The Voltaires performing at the Colony. It never occurred to us to preserve our sound for posterity. In a perfect world, we could time travel back and relive those vintage performances. I have a feeling that we might've been better than we thought.

CHAPTER TWO
WHAT SEEDS AM I SOWING?

SOLD MY ELECTRIC GUITAR AND amplifier and didn't play at all for several years. My musical interests were now devoted to listening to the sounds of Motown. Like most of my friends, I acquired a massive record collection of all the popular soul artists. On Saturdays, all the kids flocked to CJ's Music on Cookman Avenue in Asbury Park to buy the latest albums. It feels like a million year ago, but those memories still remain intact. In general, my high school experience was a relatively smooth ride given the tumultuous changes that naturally occur during the teen years. I had many friends, a stable family life, and excelled in my studies. With an additional focus on sports and girls, it was a very balanced and normal upbringing.

It was during college that I removed my old acoustic guitar from its dusty case and reinvented myself in the image of my new hero, Bob Dylan. I memorized every chord progression and lyric from his expansive songbook and even began writing my own songs. Unlike high school, college unexpectedly became a time of turmoil and rebellion. The social upheaval of those years is hard to communicate to people not of that generation. In general, it was one big blur. It straddled the late sixties and early seventies, and the priorities were not spelled out very clearly. Some people slipped through unscathed, but many of us were wanderers lost in the wilderness of our newfound freedom. University of Virginia, George Washington University, Monmouth College—three schools in five years, two cross-country trips to California, and a useless degree in philosophy summed up my personal journey. Not exactly a straight line to the top for the former honor student who had carried heavy expectations on his shoulders since birth.

A preoccupation with music dominated those years, often at the expense of academic responsibilities. What eventually became known as classic rock was a lifeline that kept legions of alienated students afloat. Massive collections of albums with psychedelic covers were like wallpaper plastering college dorm rooms as the sweet smell of pot wafted through the halls.

This was the infamous "Free Love" era, and that provided an additional deterrent to embracing the studies we were sent there to do. Pleasure-seeking became the driving force as drugs, music, and the allure of uninhibited college coeds dominated our day-to-day lives. It was a time of loose morals in a ripe environment, and like many, I found myself involved with one young woman after another. Some turned into relationships of some duration, but most liaisons were merely stoned-out one-night stands. On the one hand, I'm not particularly proud of my behavior during that phase of my life, and yet part of me wishes I could time travel back to it.

My academic pursuits obviously suffered from all these distractions, and my former status as an elite student with a promising future soon became a distant memory. I believe this time period was a critical inflection point for me. I had now officially stumbled off the beaten path and into parts unknown.

In the early 1970s, when hitchhiking was still a common practice, I hitchhiked cross-country during a summer vacation with my girlfriend, Carol. That was a little dicey at times, but we made it safely to the West Coast without being abducted by the road warriors who trolled the highways and byways of the Southwest. Dealing with the daily hardships of a trip like this, Carol and I began to get on each other's nerves. This was unfamiliar territory for us and proved to be a difficult trend to reverse. As a result, we broke up on the streets of San Francisco. After we had gone our separate ways, I started having second thoughts and tried unsuccessfully to find her, which caused me great distress. She said she was going home to Wisconsin, more than 2,000 miles away. Feeling desperate, I impulsively proceeded to hitchhike up the West Coast through Northern California, Oregon, and Washington, all the way to Vancouver, Canada. From there, I headed east through the Canadian Rockies, all the while nursing a broken heart. I was only twenty-two years old, broke, and in emotional pain. The loneliness of that journey took a toll on me. I reentered the US in Sault Ste. Marie, Michigan, and worked my way to Milwaukee, where I miraculously found Carol. Unfortunately, we couldn't recapture the magic of when we'd first met. Once it's gone, it's hard to get it back. After that realization sank in, I hitchhiked back to New Jersey to try and finish my fractured college education. Looking back, I still can't believe I did that.

I was not the only one who got sidetracked by the social upheaval of the late sixties and early seventies. The counterculture spawned revolutionaries, musical geniuses, spiritual seekers, and countless drug-related casualties. It was a miracle that so many survived amid so much recklessness and uncertainty. And during all of this, thousands of young men were drafted and sent to Vietnam to fight the spread of Communism. Many did not return. I watched in horror as twisted old men wearing bow ties conducted a bizarre draft lottery on national television. They randomly drew numbers based on your date of birth to determine who went and who stayed. My favorable number allowed me to sit in the safety of a classroom as opposed to lying in a jungle under attack from enemy fire. Opposition to the war led to widespread protests on college campuses, resulting in violence and even death. The generational divide ran deep. The Vietnam War represented the dark side of an era ironically symbolized by the peace sign.

Meanwhile, the musical thread that had run through my life continued after those misspent college years finally came to an end. My dream of a career as a songwriter began in earnest after I somehow relocated to Murray, Kentucky. This avocation occupied many hours in my loosely scheduled days, now spent living on a farm out in the country. When there was physical work to be done such as chopping wood, cutting tobacco, or hauling hay, I was always available. But my passion was my acoustic guitar and the countless songs that flowed from it. I would start with a simple chord progression, and the melody and lyrics would follow. I was still not a guitar virtuoso, but I had come a long way from playing "Sleepwalk" at the Colony. I developed a distinctive style with an affinity for the evocative minor seventh chords. Inspired by Bob Dylan, lyrics just coursed through my arm and then from my hand into a pen and onto paper. It was a cool process that felt like pure inspiration. "What Seeds Am I Sowing?" was the title of my best composition. I preserved those gems in a special notebook, but somewhere along the way it got lost and many of those songs vanished forever.

Luckily, a number of songs were memorialized in sessions at a local recording studio. I invited other musicians to join me and improvise as they saw fit. At that time, recordings were done on cassettes, of which I still have a few. Since they are now more than forty years old, they have become as fragile as papyrus.

I took my demos to Nashville, which was about two hours away. I was daydreaming that some big shot would recognize my talent and sign me to a lucrative songwriting contract. I walked up and down Music Row, cold calling on executives who were just waiting for someone like me to barge in on them. Unfortunately, the "Foghorn Leghorn" tone of my singing voice was more of an impediment than I realized. I could never get those big shots to listen to any song for more than ten seconds!

Meanwhile, I had become friendly with a local Jersey Shore legend named Phil Petillo. He was a craftsman so talented that he built his signature cutaway guitars for Bruce Springsteen, Jon Bon

Jovi, Jim Croce, and others. Everybody went to him for repair work and to buy the incredible guitar strings he had invented. He became a nationally recognized luthier par excellence. As an aside, a friend of mine read this last line and exclaimed out loud, "What the fuck is a luthier?"

I knew that Phil was a born-again Christian, and he knew that I was Jewish. Because of his evangelical beliefs, my heritage meant something special to him. It wasn't like I was the only Jew around, but when I said I was going to live in Israel, his eyes lit up. Because of my long hair, beard, and the fact that I was a Jewish carpenter, Phil secretly suspected that I was the Messiah. Even geniuses can be mistaken.

A couple of years later, I was out walking in an Israeli field near the Mediterranean Sea and came across a fallen olive tree lying in my path. I cut it up into blocks of wood in the carpentry shop on my kibbutz. Olive wood is really hard, and I thought it might be useful in the construction of musical instruments. I eventually returned to the States and personally brought Phil Petillo, guitar maker extraordinaire, some olive wood from the Holy Land! The look on his face was priceless.

Phil arranged an appointment for me with a music publisher in Manhattan. Out of respect for Phil, the executive graciously listened to my tapes. Then he said to me, "You see these shelves of demo tapes on the wall? This is all good stuff that will never get published. What artist could you imagine recording one of your songs?"

He had me there—I couldn't answer his question. Reality finally penetrated my thick skull. Songwriting could always be a hobby, but it would never be my career.

CHAPTER THREE
WESTERN KENTUCKY

IT WAS UNPLANNED THAT MY future would become harnessed to carrying heavy materials to skilled tradesmen who would assemble them into useful structures. My higher education did not yield the desired results, and at twenty-four, I suddenly found myself needing money just to live. Unskilled labor was a position that was usually available, and although I was a skinny kid from a family who valued academics, I was ready to get my hands dirty. My parents' dreams of my becoming some hotshot lawyer had fallen by the wayside. My dream of becoming a successful songwriter had likewise turned to dust. The dream world soon became the real world.

It was directly after college that I somehow landed in Murray, Kentucky, which is not far from Paris, Tennessee. The comparisons of Paris,

Tennessee to Paris, France are probably limited to the French toast you can order at Sonny's Diner. This place could've been a popular location for participants in the Witness Protection Program. If you lived out there, you were hard to find.

I moved down to Western Kentucky upon graduating in 1973 with a virtually useless degree in philosophy. I used to joke that my parents were disappointed when they heard that the "Big Philosophy Companies" weren't hiring. Opting out of law school, I impulsively accepted a friend's invitation to move down to this unlikely destination. My friend, Bob, had graduated from Murray State University and was now living on a farm with his girlfriend somewhere out in the country.

I drove into the Heartland with my clothes, guitar, and my faithful dog, Luke. After a 700-mile ride, I pulled down some long gravel road as per Bob's directions. I spotted this isolated farmhouse and pulled onto the grass driveway. I looked around and took a deep breath. I wasn't quite sure what I was getting into, but I figured I'd just go with the flow. After all, it wasn't like I was moving onto the *Spahn Ranch* with the *Manson Family!*

It had a fireplace, a well, and electricity. It did not have running water. There was an outhouse in the back. This was a far cry from the normal conveniences that I always took for granted, but after a brief period of acclimation, I came to appreciate the lifestyle in Western Kentucky. I liked chopping firewood in the winter. I liked that everyone planted a vegetable garden in the spring. I liked that when you passed somebody on a country road, they waved at you.

Bob had two dogs—Mole and Noah. Mole was part Labrador with an off-white coat with some light brown markings on his forehead. He exuded a certain strength and dignity. Noah was kind of a goofball of indeterminate breeding. And, of course, there was my dog, Luke, who was a prince among canines—highly intelligent, good-natured, and beautiful in appearance. Basically, all the same qualities exhibited by his master!

When I first arrived at Bob's farm, I got out of my car and stretched my back. I let Luke out of the car and within a flash some dog came tearing around the corner from the back of the house. Instantly, this burly white dog and Luke were going at it. I had never seen Luke in a fight before or even seen him so much as snarl at another dog. This must've been some canine territorial shit. I reached to grab Luke by the scruff of his neck and the white dog bit me on the hand. What the fuck! By now Bob had come out and pulled his dog away. Great start to this trip. I landed in the emergency room ten miles away at the University Hospital. I did not require the dreaded series of rabies shots, so at least I caught a break there. That was my introduction to Mole, whom I grew to like quite a bit in spite of our rocky start. After that initial incident, all the dogs settled in and lived like family. In fact, the area we lived in was known as Dog Creek.

After meeting some of Bob's friends and becoming familiar with the area, I soon began seeking employment. My work efforts would extend to hauling hay, masonry labor, carpentry labor, and that gladiator arena of physical exertion—cutting tobacco. Bent over those oily plants with a small hatchet, cutting down the thick stalks in one fell swoop, the sun getting hotter with every passing hour—this was backbreaking work. If someone had told me ten years earlier that I'd end up doing this, I'd have said they were out of their mind.

"Boss, taking off here!" That's a line from *Cool Hand Luke* when chain gang prisoners sought permission to remove their shirts because of the sweltering heat. This job wasn't quite as oppressive as that. In fact, our "bosses" were local farmers who were some of the nicest people I've ever met. They were not stereotypical rednecks with crew cuts and narrow points of view. They saw past our long hair and beards and showed respect and appreciation for our honest efforts.

One of them innocently asked me, "Charles, are you a Jew?"

"Yes, Ernest," I replied.

He followed up with, "I thought you were Jewish or Italian. Are you a full-blooded Jew?"

"Yes, Ernest."

He added, "It seems to me there's a genuine Jew lives over to Mayfield."

The sheer innocence of this line of questioning made me smile. Had I been a full-blooded Cherokee, I would not have garnered this much scrutiny. I was kind of a curiosity to them, but they respected my work ethic on a job that slaves had done a hundred years earlier. They viewed me with a degree of reverence owing to their Southern Baptist beliefs. I wasn't the Messiah, but I was the closest thing they had ever seen. After my first day on the job, the owner of the farm came up to me and said, "Charles, you're a good 'un." That simple sentence was one of the finest compliments I have ever received.

The big tobacco leaves would lie on the ground until wagons hitched to tractors arrived in the fields. You'd load the plants onto the wagons, and from there they'd head to the barn to be cured. This work has been going on in this part of the country since before the Civil War. It's a big part of the local economy, a major cash crop.

At noon, the mothers and daughters served us lunch at a picnic table filled with fried chicken, potato salad, okra, and corn bread. They would come around and graciously refill our glasses with sweet iced tea. One of the daughters had caught my eye. She was a shapely farm girl in her late teens. From my brief conversation with her, I saw that she was very sweet and very bright. I wondered what a future with a girl like that would be for a guy like me.

After lunch, we'd put our backs to the ground and rest for a short time under a shady oak tree. Fully renewed, we would head over to the barn to unload the wagons. We placed a metal spike on top of long sticks and speared the thick stalks at the base of the tobacco leaves. Each stick might end up holding about ten plants. We climbed up in the barn and hung the heavy, loaded sticks in the rafters to dry out and cure. It was kind of a primitive system, but it had passed the test of time.

Something happened one day that I'll never forget. A tractor had left a fully loaded wagon of heavy tobacco leaves at the top of an incline leading into the barn. Our crew consisted of college graduates, hippies, and carpetbaggers, all looking to earn a few bucks from this seasonal work. Our unofficial foreman was a guy named Fred Thomas. He was our age but already an experienced tobacco cutter. Fred was kind of a Renaissance man who had two very attractive sisters at Murray State University. I was fond of both of them. I guess I just liked those country girls, although that's not really relevant to this story.

Anyway, rather than wait for the tractor to return from the field to drive the tobacco into the barn, Fred decided we could manually ease the wagon down the incline to get a head start on hanging the sticks. There were six of us—two on each side, one at the front, and Fred at the bottom. We slowly pushed the heavy wagon forward. As the center of the wagon passed the fulcrum of the incline, we felt it getting away from us and tried to use our bodies like human brakes to slow it down. The guy at the top who was trying to pull it backward fell down, and Fred tried to pit himself against the bottom of the wagon with all his might. We couldn't stop it. The guys on the other side fell away in order not to get run over by the rolling wheels, and I jumped out of the way too. Fred got slammed by the force of the runaway wagon against the wall of the barn.

Oh, my God! Is Fred dead? was all I could think in that moment. We ran down and saw that he was trapped but still conscious. Miraculously, it was the corner of the runaway wagon that crashed into the wall first, such that the full brunt of it didn't crush his ribcage. We pushed it back and freed Fred from the pressure. He was lucky that he wasn't crippled for life. We all sat down on the ground and just silently stared into space for a long while. It was like a prayer vigil. I was feeling bad that I had pulled away to save myself from getting crushed beneath the wheel.

Fred, who had by now gathered himself, noticed how distraught I was. He walked over to me and said, "I think they call that Jewish guilt. Don't worry about it." I appreciated that gesture from a guy who had almost just gotten killed. After a little while, we all climbed up onto the rafters and hung out the tobacco leaves to dry.

After tobacco season ended, I went to work for a couple of country carpenters building houses. I was just a laborer learning the rudiments of carpentry, which eventually became my real career. My first boss was a builder named Guy Cunningham. He was a straight arrow Christian from Calloway County, and I was a long-haired Jew from Jersey. I was willing to work hard, and that's what counted. I carried heavy lumber and learned how to swing a hammer and operate a power saw. I liked this work, but hanging out with Evangelical Christians was a strange experience for me. They had a sense of humor, but it was much more prim and proper than the ball-breaking I was accustomed to. I'd grown up with wisecracking Italians, Irish, and Jews, whereas Guy Cunningham lived among Southern Baptists, who probably got their laughs joking about the peach cobbler at the church social and shit like that.

When I wasn't working, I spent a lot of time taking long walks all over Dog Creek. On one snowy day, I walked several miles across some fields and streams to visit some people I knew. The dogs went with me, with Luke taking the lead and scouting the area ahead. The snow was deep and the footing uneasy. Noah kept getting stuck and struggled to keep up. Mole followed about twenty yards behind, guarding our flank. When I would stop walking, I'd look back and Mole would also stop and just look at me. He was a good dog.

That spring Bob went back to New Jersey for a week to visit his folks. It was a rainy night. Luke and Noah were hanging out on the screened-in back porch. Mole had been sick, so he was sitting inside with me. I was listening to some music, drinking a Scotch, and staring at the fireplace. Mole suddenly stood up as if to get closer to the fire, then he just stopped and keeled over on his side. He was dead. I tried to calmly absorb what had just transpired. I gathered my wits and realized I had to bury Mole. There was a small cemetery behind the outhouse. It was raining pretty hard out, so I called a friend of mine who lived nearby to give me a hand. Without hesitation, Russell got into his pickup truck and came right over. We dug as deep and wide a hole as we could before we hit some rock. We dumped some lime into the hole and then lowered Mole into it. We filled the dirt back in and covered his grave with stones. Then we went inside and drank some Scotch. The next day I made a little sign and nailed it to two stakes. It read: *Here Lies Mole—a Noble Creature and Loyal Friend.* I hammered it deep into the ground at the head of his grave. I wonder if it's still there.

When Bob went back to New Jersey to visit his family, his girlfriend, Mary, remained behind on the farm. She was a buxom, blonde-haired, blue-eyed art student at Murray State University. Mary and I didn't really get along that well. When suddenly you just show up, even though you've been invited, you are now the third wheel in the household and that can be a recipe for tension.

We had planted a big vegetable garden in the backyard, as most folks did down there. I enjoyed working in it—tilling the soil, planting the seedlings, hoeing the rows of tomatoes, corn, beans, and squash. It was outdoor physical work that was gratifying, especially when the vegetables reached the edible stage.

Mary also liked working in the garden. In Bob's absence, we did that together. Laboring individually in silence, we reached a point of relative harmony. With the hot sun beating down on us, we went inside to drink some iced tea. During our break, we put some music on the record player. I don't know exactly how it happened, but we just started dancing, and before I knew it, we were in each other's arms. We were young, and healthy, and sweaty from our physical exertion in the garden. Maybe our prior resentments were masking some sexual attraction, but now we gave into our desires like wild animals. Without inhibition or guilt, we made love nonstop for the next week. We did it in the bed where Mary and Bob had slept. We did it in the woods, and we did it right in the dirt in the garden. The intimacy and excitement were only enhanced by the fact that it was forbidden and temporary. Lustful affairs were not uncommon in the days of our youth, especially when desire met opportunity.

When Mary got a call from Bob that he was on his way back from Jersey, I volunteered to pick him up at the bus station. He stepped off the bus as I waited in my car. Without any forethought, I immediately told him what had occurred. I guess I thought honesty was the best policy no matter the consequences. Bob was understandably thrown by this surprising confession, but he wasn't angry. In fact, he seemed appreciative that I had told him up front rather than hide it from him.

We drove for thirty minutes in silence until we arrived back at the farm. I decided to stay out of the way and let Bob and Mary sort things out. I stayed in my room upstairs, but it quickly became apparent that this arrangement was no longer tenable. I moved in with some friends down the road.

We were all part of the same community of young people living out in the country. We shared a lot of activities together—working, partying, playing music, and so on. Bob and Mary tried to make a go of it, but it was never the same. Likewise, I could feel a gnawing passive aggression from Bob toward me whenever we saw each other. I couldn't blame him, but I didn't feel guilty. Mary and I were young, healthy, and horny, and we had been left alone in the middle of nowhere. She and I remained cordial but never pursued any further dalliance. In fact, we never spoke of it again. She eventually moved back to Chicago and life went on as before.

After Mole died, I mostly just walked with Luke—sometimes up in the hills, sometimes down by the stream, and sometimes down the narrow gravel road that went from one end of the valley to the other. We were out on that desolate road one day when some car I didn't recognize came driving up slowly. I approached it warily. Luke had run down into the meadow below, chasing some critter. There were four men in the car, and they looked like some of the inbred people that were scattered around the area. Most of the folks around there were kindhearted Southern Baptists, but this crew was not them. They were rough-looking, semitoothless rednecks who had stumbled across a longhaired, bearded Jewish guy out on a lonely back road. Of course, they didn't know I was Jewish. I'd be willing to bet they had never met a Jew in their life. In any event, I thought this could be a dangerous situation. Were they drinking moonshine in the car? Were those shotguns lying on their laps?

They asked me where the General Store was in New Concord. I told them to hang a left at the end of the gravel road. One guy in the back seat, with his hat pulled down low, was eyeballing me with bad intentions. I saw that movie *Deliverance*, and I was getting ready to run down into the meadow to get Luke and try to make it home. Instead, they nodded and slowly drove on. Luke and I started walking back on the road. My fear was that I would suddenly hear gravel churning and turn to see that old car coming back. It didn't happen. Disaster averted.

Growing up, we never had a dog. In fact, it was never even mentioned. I think my mother just assumed that a dog would track dirt into the house. I'm sure she couldn't ever imagine taking it for a walk or even opening a can of dog food. And God forbid, what would she do if the dog shit right in front of her? This was definitely not for her.

Luke was the second dog I'd owned in my life. The first was a German shepherd named Lumpy. I was still in college at the time and had driven up to Syracuse University to visit an old girlfriend. For some reason, this big dog just started following us around. We called the phone number on his tags but the person who answered claimed to have no knowledge of this dog. I have never figured that part of the story out. At the conclusion of the weekend, I headed back to New Jersey with this big German shepherd sitting in the back seat of my car. I could see him in my rearview mirror, and it made me smile. I named him Lumpy after a character in the old TV series *Leave It to Beaver*.

This was a big responsibility for a generally misguided college student in the '70s. I had been staying at my parents' house during spring break when I returned from Syracuse with this huge German shepherd in tow. Lumpy had a heart of gold and soon won my parents over. My mother, however, equated dog food with dog shit, so every time I fed him a can of food, I had to immediately take the garbage out. We had a big yard, and Lumpy would lie around under an oak tree while I mindlessly played Dylan songs on my guitar. We were quite a pair of misfits. My parents used to stare at us out the window, wondering what such a once-promising young man would do with his future. It was like a scene out of *The Graduate*. Their big question would be answered soon enough but not the way they thought.

Eventually I took Lumpy back to the suburbs of Virginia where I was living with a bunch of guys while attending George Washington University. Lumpy fit right in with this group of laid-back underachievers. He was perfectly content to just lie on the floor watching TV with us. But on the days when I drove out into the country, he would spring into action and run like the wind. He was like two different dogs—one minute he was *The Big Lebowski* and the next minute he was *Seabiscuit*. It was beautiful to watch him come to life when he was set free in some pasture to run and jump to his heart's content.

The next year I was planning an open-ended trip to California. My parents couldn't handle taking care of Lumpy, so I took him to my sister's house outside of Boston. My little niece and nephew loved him, and I have photos of them hugging this big gentle dog around the neck. Unfortunately, Lumpy had a natural antipathy toward mailmen. This is common with many dogs, some kind of territorial thing. One day he went too far and bit the mailman. That effectively ended his time in Massachusetts.

My cousin Andrea said that her friend in New Jersey would love to have Lumpy come live with her family. It seemed like a good match. They had kids and a house with a backyard, and it felt right. A year later, I returned and went to visit Lumpy at their house in Long Branch. It broke my heart. He was outside, in a small caged-in area in the rear. He looked old and gaunt, his eyes as empty as a prisoner from Dachau. I don't recall interacting with those people. It was probably best that I didn't. I blamed myself and have never forgotten it.

A couple of years later, I got my second dog, Lucas (a.k.a. Luke). I was now attending the third school in my illustrious college career and living back on the Jersey Shore. I had picked up a hitchhiker on Ocean Avenue who was holding this black, gray, and brown puppy. He said the dog was part German shepherd, part Australian shepherd, and part dingo (a wild dog from Australia descended from wolves). He mentioned that he was going away and needed to find the dog a home. I dropped the guy off a couple of miles down the road, and suddenly I was the proud owner of a six-week-old puppy of exotic pedigree. I learned later that his distinctive tricolor coat was called blue merle. Whenever I see someone walking a dog with a blue merle coat, I think back to Luke. I still pat myself on the back for responsibly raising this fine animal, who turned out to be one of the greatest dogs in the history of the world!

Upon graduation, I moved from my ramshackle beachfront tenement to the aforementioned farm in Kentucky. In New Jersey, Luke had spent countless hours tracking down sticks I would toss into the ocean. Living out in the country, he ran free and never needed to be on a leash or in any enclosure. He went for long walks with me in the scenic countryside or did his own thing when I was doing mine.

Once, in the winter, I put on my heavy coat and walked out to this hidden meadow. It was so peaceful and quiet there that I actually lay down in the snow. I could feel my back against the frozen earth and see the cumulus clouds above. Luke just sat next to me in an alert posture as if standing guard. Occasionally he would take off for a while and then return to check on me. This might sound foreign to some people, but in retrospect, it was one of the most peaceful experiences I can ever recall.

After four years, I was planning a trip to Israel. In Western Kentucky, I was basically the only Jew in the county. I loved living the country life, but I wanted to experience it among my ancestral tribe. I did not know how long I would be gone for. I needed to make sure that Luke had a safe and secure place to stay. I did not want what happened to Lumpy to be repeated. The other people on our farm said Luke could keep living there. I trusted them and agreed.

Some years later I returned for a visit. I was told that Luke was living with a family on a neighboring farm. I drove there and stopped at the head of their long gravel driveway. I spotted this older version of Luke playing on the lawn, naturally with a stick. There were some kids playing alongside him. I instinctively called out his name, and he lifted his head up. I called it again, and he started running toward me. The audio memory of dogs is amazing. He ran right into me. He knew who had raised him, and it was so gratifying that he remembered me. I introduced myself to the owners of the farm. They were good country folk who obviously loved Luke. I could see that he had a good life there. I wanted to take him back, but I knew that was not happening. I drove away with a full heart—the exact opposite of the despair I'd felt after leaving Lumpy in that hellhole. Other dogs have been ruined for me by the high standard set by those two resplendent four-legged titans. I've never owned another dog since.

CHAPTER FOUR

THE HOLY LAND

MY FATHER PASSED AWAY FROM Lou Gehrig's disease when I was twenty-five. He was only fifty-nine years old. It made no sense. He had been healthy his whole life and then was suddenly stricken with a debilitating disease for which there was no cure. That was over forty years ago, and there still is no cure for this rare attack on the nervous system, technically called Amyotrophic Lateral Sclerosis, or ALS. The doctors never could determine how he got it. Maybe it was from residual lead in the enemy bullets that wounded him on the beaches of Anzio in Italy during World War II. If that was the cause, it took decades for the poison to fully leach in and terminally disable him.

My parents had sold the big house with the big yard that I had grown up in several years earlier. They then moved into a two-bedroom apartment in Asbury Park while I was living on a farm in Kentucky. They asked me to come home to help out. When I first arrived, my father came to the door to let me in. We looked at each other, and he started to cry and ran away. I'll never forget it. It was heartbreaking to watch my father fade away because of some illness nobody could understand. I remember having to carry him into the shower and holding him up so he wouldn't fall as the water sprayed over him. It still brings tears to my eyes almost fifty years later.

I was twenty-seven when I finalized my plans to go to Israel, two years after my father's passing. I have no doubt that his death played a big part in my decision to go. I would not have embarked on such a bold adventure during his illness. His passing was a line of demarcation that inspired me to chase my dreams while I still could. My entire inheritance was $800 from a mutual fund he had purchased in my name, and with that money, I bought an open-ended round-trip ticket to Israel that was good for up to a year. I had thought about this trip for quite some time, and now it was becoming a reality. I made my arrangements through the Jewish Agency in New York. They would send me to a kibbutz to work as a volunteer. I would be traveling alone, and I didn't know a single soul living there. I felt excited about this new adventure but also a little anxious. This was different from cross-country trips during summer vacations from college or even moving down to Kentucky.

The direct flight from Newark to Tel Aviv normally took about twelve hours, but for some reason, we were forced to land in Frankfurt, Germany, and the airline put us up in a hotel for the night. They would send a bus to pick us up the following morning. My seat on the flight was next to an older gentleman from Iran. He had been visiting family in the States and was moving to Israel. I figured he was about sixty. He wore a rumpled suit with an old-fashioned hat and spoke broken English. We attempted to converse, but it was like a wrestling match that went nowhere. His natural language was Persian, or technically Farsi. He seemed confused by the change in our travel itinerary as the concierge led us to the elevator in the hotel. I told him the bus would be picking us up at nine the next morning, and he went to his room just down the hall from mine.

I went down to the bar and drank a beer and ate some schnitzel, then walked in the night air in Frankfurt, Germany. It felt a little surreal. Only a few hours earlier, I had been boarding a flight in New York, and now I found myself strolling through a park in Frankfurt. I headed back to the hotel, watched the news on some German TV station, and fell asleep.

Awakened from a dream by knocking on my door, I looked at the clock. It was 5:00 a.m. *What the fuck is this?*

I put on my pants and stumbled to the door. Standing there was my new friend, the Iranian Jew. He was dressed in his suit and hat and holding his suitcase. He looked like the Persian version of Buster Keaton. He was all ready to go. I managed to explain to him that the bus wouldn't be there for another four hours, then watched him walk back down the hall to his room. I felt like I had inherited this guy as a result of a random seating chart by El Al Airlines. I felt bad that he had gotten confused, but our language barrier made it difficult to communicate. Meanwhile, I had a lot on my mind with all the uncertainty of this new undertaking. I attempted to go back to sleep but without success.

We finally landed at Ben Gurion Airport outside of Tel Aviv. The air was warm and felt good. Feeling kind of disoriented, I walked around for a while and then hailed a cab to take me to my preplanned destination, Kibbutz Beit Alfa. Beit Alfa was the first kibbutz in Israel, founded in 1922 by Zionists from Poland and Lithuania. It was located in the Beit Sh'ean Valley near the town of Afula, in the shadow of Mount Gilboa. If moving to Kentucky had been a half-baked idea, then this decision was even more radical. At this point in my life, I was supposed to be a successful attorney with a wife and kid and a dog! How did such a normal guy drift so far off the beaten track?

I stared out the window in a dreamy state during the hour-long ride through the Israeli countryside. It looked beautiful. My map showed that Beit Alfa was not far from the Jordan River and the West Bank. It would be a confluence of Jewish settlers and Arab residents living in a state of separation and controlled tension.

As we got closer, I spotted a big complex hemmed in by barbed wire and asked the driver if that was Kibbutz Beit Alfa. He told me that was a high-security prison that housed Palestinian terrorists. Nice. The thought of living in proximity to imprisoned terrorists bent on destroying Israel was a bit unsettling.

We eventually drove through a guarded gate into a beautifully landscaped area where the driver pulled over. He said, "*B'hatzlika,*" meaning good luck. I would need it. I paid him and thanked him, then he drove away. I stood there alone with my bags for a moment, wondering to myself, *Now what have I done?*

I located the office where they processed volunteers like me. The woman in charge was somehow gruff and friendly at the same time. I ultimately was led to my new living quarters and given sheets and towels and work clothes. There was no bathroom in my room. The common toilet and shower were pointed out to me as well as the community dining room. Dinner was in two hours. I thought to myself, *One step at a time.* It's funny—over forty years later, and I'm still living one step at a time.

My earliest impressions of Kibbutz Beit Alfa were mixed. On the one hand, it was located in a gorgeous valley with flowers and trees and hills. It was a little bit like Kentucky in that respect. But the people seemed strange to me. I didn't know any Israelis in the States. In the dining room, I studied the residents as they filed in. The men had the same Semitic faces as my parents' friends, but the similarities pretty much ended there. My great-grandfather, Abraham Levinsohn, had left Lithuania in 1893 to escape the Russian pogroms and landed in New York. I've wondered if he ever considered going to Palestine instead. Had he taken that path, I might never have been born.

This kibbutz was essentially a socialist society founded on physical labor. In fifty years, Beit Alfa had flourished as a result of that hard work. It was a microcosm of a renaissance sparked by an influx of Eastern European idealists in the 1920s. They overcame malaria-infested swamps, barren deserts, and Palestinian marauders to create a thriving society.

I may be a Jew, but I still couldn't quite comprehend how I had gotten there. I was in the fucking

Middle East! I might as well have landed on the surface of the moon!

I may have been quiet by nature, but I wasn't shy. The experiences in my early twenties gave me the confidence to relate to people from different backgrounds. If I could get along with rednecks in the fields of Kentucky, then I should be able to get along with opinionated Jews in the Beit Sh'ean Valley.

The volunteer workers were a mix of Americans, Europeans, Russians, and South Africans. I spotted a table where they were eating. I imagine it was like on the first day in prison, when one would intuitively recognize where they belong. Unlike in those prison movies, there would be no tattooed Aryan Nation assholes in this dining hall. There might have been tattoos on the wrists of some of the older members there, but they were applied under different circumstances altogether.

The dining room was cafeteria-style, and I would have to adjust to the Mediterranean diet—hummus, olives, salads, meats, and breads. I got my tray and filled up a plate, taking some of the meat even though I didn't know what it was. Turkey maybe? I asked someone and was told it was called *steak lavon*, which means white steak and is actually pork. For my first meal on a kibbutz in Israel, I ate pork for dinner. I didn't even eat pork in the States!

I sat down and ate my first meal with some of the other volunteers, quickly noticing there were some good-looking European girls in the group. Those blonde blue-eyed Danish girls looked nice. If I just smiled and turned on the old Kentucky charm, maybe one of them might fall for me. In fact, I did have a fling with Monique from Copenhagen. European girls were just different from American girls. It's hard to explain.

The next day was my first day at work. I had to report to a meeting place at 6:00 a.m. to ride in a wagon out to the grapefruit orchards, or *pardess*. I was supposed to be wearing the blue work clothes they'd given me, but I didn't like them, and so I wore my own jeans and a T-shirt. That was probably a mistake, as I sensed some of the Israelis glancing at me and speaking secretively to each other in Hebrew. I was already a pariah, and they didn't even know me yet!

They gave me a little ladder and a bucket and said I was to climb up into the trees and remove the grapefruits. The orchards seemed to go on forever. This was a job that would never end. I immediately hated it. I was used to more dynamic work, like building houses. But I had signed up, and so I had to make the best of it.

I ended up on the edge of the orchard by a barbed wire fence. I took a little break to eat one of the grapefruits or *eshcoliot*. They were huge and ruby red on the inside. I cut it in half and ate a section. It was the best grapefruit I had ever eaten. Unbelievably juicy and tasty. Suddenly, on the other side of the barbed wire, a young Arab guy appeared. He motioned to me to give him a grapefruit. Without hesitation, I pushed the other half of mine through the fence to him. It was so big that I couldn't finish it. He looked at me in disappointment that I did not give him a whole piece of fruit and wandered off. I felt lucky he didn't come back and kill me.

After a while, the Israelis started to warm up to me. I had extricated myself from picking grapefruits and landed a job in the fishponds, or *midgeh*. This was the hardest physical work on the kibbutz. You got up at dawn and raked in heavy loads of fish in big nets that required the arm power of seven or eight guys. Having survived all that slave labor in Kentucky, my hands were calloused and my muscles were strong, so this was more my style, and I immediately rose to the challenge. The crew included some of the toughest guys on the kibbutz, and although I didn't speak Hebrew, most of them could speak English. As opposed to all the Christians I toiled with in those tobacco fields, everybody here was Jewish. When the hot sun is bearing down on you and the loads are getting heavy, you tend to forget about all of that.

The way you gain acceptance on a kibbutz is by your ability to work, and I succeeded in that arena. It also didn't hurt that I could play a musical instrument. I had brought my old guitar, which had been reconditioned by my old friend, Phil Petillo. I found other guitarists, and we jammed under the stars on those warm summer nights. This is a universally galvanizing pastime. It is also a magnet for women who are attracted to the sensibilities of musicians. Fishing during the day and playing music at night—I had become a true Renaissance Man! My initial period of alienation in Israel had passed, at least temporarily.

After about six months, I got the opportunity to enroll in a program to study Hebrew as well as work, so I relocated to Kibbutz Maagan Michael. This was a bigger community that housed about a thousand residents, and it was on the Mediterranean Sea, south of Haifa. Since I'd grown up as a beach boy, this seemed like a natural fit. It was also a very affluent place because, in addition to all the agricultural enterprises, they had also built a plastics factory that shipped irrigation fittings all over the world. Unlike at Beit Alfa, I had to share a room with two other enrollees, which kind of sucked. They were nice enough guys—one was from South Africa, the other from Southern California.

I was initially assigned to work on the banana plantation. This was a heavy lifting job. I didn't hate it, but having previously worked on a tobacco plantation, I once again I felt like an African slave working in the jungle for White masters. The fruit grows on eight-foot-tall trees in bunches of about thirty bananas. When they are ripe, some tall Israeli guy with a machete chops the bunch loose from the tree. My job was to stand underneath it and let it land on my shoulder. Then I had to run through the jungle with it and place it on a wagon and rush back for the next bunch. I heard there were big spiders residing among those bananas, but fortunately I never saw any.

After a couple of hours, wagons took us back to the dining hall to wash up and eat a hearty breakfast. The crews from different branches of work all ate separately with their coworkers. I spotted some guys wearing rubber overalls, indicating that they worked in the fishponds—my old job at Beit Alfa. I liked that job and hoped to eventually join them. Some older residents piled in wearing their blue work clothes and this funny looking hat called a *kova temble* (clown's hat). Again, I saw in them the Jewish-looking faces of my father's friends. Had their forebears taken a different turn, they might have spent their whole lives as businessmen on the Jersey Shore.

After breakfast, we continued cutting and carrying bananas until lunch. Then after a meal and a short rest, I went to the classroom to learn Hebrew.

The goal of all of this was to get you to permanently move to Israel, or, as it was called, to *make Aliyah*. I planned to stay for the full year that my plane ticket allowed and then go back to the States. This was meant to be just another adventure in my already unconventional life.

I finished the study program and then got transferred to work in the fishponds full time. The head of this unit was an ex-commando, Ami Eshel. He was some kind of hero in the last war and supposedly swam underwater and attached explosives to the hulls of enemy ships. There were several other commando types working there, plus me—a peace-loving, guitar-playing, ex-hippie by way of the Jersey Shore and Western Kentucky. By this time, I spoke rudimentary Hebrew, and that helped in the assimilation process. They do a lot of screaming in this branch of work, so my delicate sensibilities would have to be placed on hold.

We'd usually meet at six in the morning, in a small building where we changed into rubber waders in the winter or bathing suits and sneakers in the summer. Somebody made a pot of Turkish coffee, which was called *botz*, meaning mud. It was thick and strong, and I liked it.

We'd head out in wagons and trucks to one of the twenty man-made ponds Ami determined would be our work location for the day. This was fish farming, or aquaculture as it's known in the

States. The fish are raised in irrigated ponds about an acre or so in size. When they reach maturity, they are harvested in big nets and placed in tanks on the backs of trucks and shipped fresh to markets in Israeli cities. It was hard, physical, dirty work. I was already strong, but this kind of effort taxed different muscles in the body. I loved it.

We'd break for breakfast around nine and ride over to the community dining hall overlooking the Mediterranean. Then we'd go back and work for a few more hours until lunch and for several hours after that. It was probably about a ten-hour workday.

I felt a certain amount of pride about being a member of this crew. Everybody in the whole place worked hard, but this branch was acknowledged as the most physically demanding of all the jobs. The kids all admired you, and the young women looked at you differently. I wouldn't go so far as to say that we were rock stars, but it still felt cool to be a part of it.

I remember in the summer, the subtropical heat would be brutal. At the end of the workday, we occasionally piled into a tractor-pulled wagon and rode along the Mediterranean beach and then up a twisting gravel road. At the top was a big concrete pipe about three feet in diameter. This was an offshoot of the intricate irrigation system that fed all the fishponds. The source was a tributary of the

Zarqa River, which was the second-largest river in Israel after the Jordan River. The Zarqa ran north and south through the center of the country and had tributaries that ran east and west. This one cut through the Carmel Mountains and passed by the Arab town of Binyamina and finally landed in this concrete pipe on a hill above our beach.

We were all caked in mud and brackish water and weary from pulling nets all day in the hot sun. We took turns standing under the wide pipe as someone turned the large wheel that released the water. I remember that it was freezing cold and clear, and it landed on you with some force. I would stand under it for a few minutes and look out at the sea and the sky, feeling like I was being baptized in holy water of the Holy Land. I felt pure and clean. It was the most refreshing feeling I think I've ever known.

Meanwhile I was getting tired of sharing a room with two other guys. I was working hard and felt I was entitled to at least some basic comforts. I also craved some privacy just in case I wanted to bring one of those European beauties back to my room. As it turned out, one of my coworkers in the *midgeh* had just begun his army service. Amiron Berkovich had a small apartment with a bathroom and refrigerator in it, and he graciously told me I could stay there while he was gone. When he would periodically come home for a weekend, I would clear out and go back to my old room so he could relax. This was an improvement in my quality of life, and I appreciated Amiron's generosity.

One day at 5:30 in the morning, I was headed to work and some woman named Michal, who was in charge of the housing committee, stopped me and told me that I could no longer stay in Amiron's apartment. Apparently, his parents objected to anyone using his place even when he wasn't there. I cleared out, and when I saw Amiron that weekend, I told him what had happened. He replied that it was perfectly fine with him for me to continue staying there. So, after the weekend, I returned there. Sure enough, later that week Michal spotted me. She approached me in the dining hall and told me I had to leave the kibbutz because of this unspeakable infraction. I was pissed off and said no problem, it's your loss. Word spread to the fishponds, and my coworkers there were not happy about this news. I was eventually summoned to the office of the head of the entire kibbutz. The guy's name was Nissim and his son Noam worked with me in the fishponds. Noam was an ex-commando and a very nice guy who enjoyed practicing his English with me. You would never guess that he had been a trained killer of enemy combatants. In any case, Nissim interrogated me about my insubordinate behavior. We spoke in Hebrew. At the end, he said, "*Ha ben sheli omar le, ani yodea davar echad, be midgeh,*

Charley mao ochuz!" Translation: "My son said to me, I know one thing, in the fishponds, Charley is 100 percent." In Israel, that is the greatest compliment an outsider can receive. My reputation at work superseded any petty disputes, so they gave me my own apartment with a bathroom. Whenever I ran into Michal after that, you would think that we were the best of friends!

I settled into the life there of getting up early, working hard, eating a healthy Mediterranean diet, and socializing at night. In the summer, I got a very deep tan from working outside all day. My hair grew long and was bleached out by the powerful rays of the sun. I have some photos of myself looking like some ancient Hebrew from Biblical times. I felt the healthiest that I ever have in my life.

After work, I routinely walked down to the beach and swam in the clear water of the Mediterranean Sea. This was a familiar connection to my life growing up on the Jersey Shore. I would burst out of the water and gaze up at the sun as I walked slowly up the beach to lie down in the sand and peacefully fall asleep. Decades later, I am still practicing this same ritual back at home as I climb out of the Atlantic Ocean late on a summer day.

There are patches on the floor of the Mediterranean that are covered with coral from some nearby reef. If you're not careful, they can cut your feet. Fortunately, my feet were quite calloused from walking around barefoot as was the habit on the kibbutz. One day the sea was unusually rough with bigger waves than normal. I took a short swim to get refreshed and then retreated back to the water's edge. Suddenly I heard someone screaming for help. It was some teenage girl from the kibbutz who had been carried out too far by the current. I jumped up and dove in, swimming as fast as I could through the waves to try to help her. I was not a particularly strong swimmer and had no lifeguard training whatsoever, but it didn't matter—I had to get to her. I reached her, she put her arms around my neck, and we fought the current together. Then we caught a lucky break as a wave took hold of us and washed us back onto shore.

We collapsed in the sand gasping for breath. Both of us had cuts on our knees and feet from the sharp coral shards. I asked her in Hebrew, "*Ot be-seder?*" (Are you okay?) She answered me in English that she was. She was dark-skinned, possibly from Yemen, and had been adopted by the kibbutz. Her name was Anat, and she was maybe sixteen or seventeen. Anyway, I asked her if she was okay to walk back. She said that she was and thanked me for helping her. I replied in Hebrew, "*Ein b'aya.*" (No problem.) She said, "*L'hitraoat.*" (See you later.)

After she left, I walked along the shoreline, hoping the salty water would help heal my battered feet. I felt uplifted by this unexpected occurrence.

I've rarely had the opportunity to feel heroic in life, and it was a strange and gratifying feeling. I knew it was temporary like all other emotions, but figured I might as well savor it while it lasted. It did get me a little extra play because Anat told all her friends about our adventure. After dinner in the outdoor café, she approached me and thanked me again. She looked very attractive in her shorts and tank top, with jet black hair and big brown eyes that were like deep pools. No, I was not going down that road, no matter how tempting. She was too young. Who knows—maybe in a fantasy world, if Anat had been a little older and I a little younger— we could've gotten married! We could have lived our whole lives together by the Mediterranean Sea, raising a family of beautiful half-Sephardic, half-Ashkenazi kids. We would tell the story of how we first met over and over again. The details of her rescue by the handsome young American would have grown into the stuff of legends!

Anyway, back on Earth, my responsibilities in the *midgeh* increased as my fluency in Hebrew improved. I occasionally drove the truck that held the tank into which we loaded the fish. I was familiar with the maze of gravel roads that intertwined the twenty ponds. Ami would tell me in Hebrew, "Charley, fill the tank with water and drive over to #18 and wait for the crew to arrive." There was an overhead pipe that I'd maneuver the truck under and then open the valve until it reached the fill line. Then I'd turn on the aerators circulating the water so that the freshly caught fish would stay alive until reaching the market.

I was driving along one sunny day and thinking to myself that this was pretty cool. This vehicle was captured from the Egyptians in the Sinai Desert during the Six-Day War. Now here I am, Charles Levinsohn from New Jersey, driving this truck along the Mediterranean coast as part of a crew that's supplying fresh fish to the people of Israel. I thought that my dearly departed father would have been proud of me. I guess I was still seeking his approval even though he had been dead for several years. As I was daydreaming about such things, I inadvertently drove the truck off the road and into a ditch. A tractor had to come and tow it out. Maybe my father was sending me a message to always remain humble. Point well taken. I would receive that same message many more times throughout my life.

I was then assigned to accompany the kibbutz driver who delivered our fish to various cities such as Tel Aviv, Haifa, and Jerusalem. I was commissioned to drive on our roads within the kibbutz but not on the highways outside of it. The driver's name was Shimon. He was kind of a rough character, short, muscular, unshaven, an Ashkenazi Jew. I figured he was about forty. He smoked a lot of cigarettes and had a surly disposition. At first when I rode with him, he didn't say a word. We'd arrive at a marketplace, and Shimon would back the truck onto a ramp where we'd unload the fish. Some guy at the bottom would weigh the load and give Shimon a receipt. My job was to climb down and open the hatch door so that the fish and water from our tank would rush down the ramp, then climb into the tank and push out any stragglers with a wide broom until it was empty. It wasn't very complicated, and I was happy to periodically get outside of the kibbutz and into the real world.

On the way back, we often stopped for lunch at one of those gas stations that had a café attached to it. The food at these places was sensational. Fresh hummus, shawarma, salads, and pita bread. We'd finish it off with some baklava and a cup of Turkish coffee. Shimon would pay with money allotted to him by the kibbutz. After a couple of these trips, Shimon grew to like me. Whereas initially he'd never spoken, now he wouldn't shut the fuck up! Whenever I would see him at dinner in the dining hall with his wife and kids, he always went out of his way to be friendly to me. I think in a way, he was proud that he and I were friends. That was nice. Small stuff like that is what I remember most.

During my three years in Israel, I visited many places. It's a small country, but there is so much to see in terms of sheer beauty and historical significance. The kibbutz organized tours, or *tiulim*, for people like me, designed to convince us to move there, or make *Aliyah*. We also watched many documentaries on the Holocaust to further add to our motivation.

At eleven o'clock in the morning on *Yom HaShoah* (Holocaust Memorial Day), a siren went off throughout the country in remembrance of the Holocaust. I was still eating breakfast in the dining hall with the fishing crew when the siren sounded. Everybody stood up for two minutes of silence. Throughout the country, everyone stood up from whatever they were doing and cars pulled over on the side of the road in observance. This one act was a totally galvanizing annual event in an otherwise contentious and argumentative nation.

During my time in Israel, I climbed Mount Sinai at dawn where Moses carried the Ten Commandments. I visited the Sea of Galilee near the city of Tiberias. I spent three days in the West Bank, observing life in the Occupied Territories. I floated in the salty water of the Dead Sea. I visited the Western Wall and the Temple Mount in the Old City of Jerusalem. I went to Beersheva, Safad, Eilat, Sharm el-Sheihk, the Golan Heights, and Yad Vashem. When I think of it now, it was the experience of a lifetime.

After forty years, I can confirm that those impressions stay in your bones even if you rarely consciously think about them. They just become part of your DNA. The further I get from it, the more it all seems like a dream, but it's a good dream that I'm grateful for.

Occasionally, the kibbutz gave us a day off during the work week. I would often walk out to the coastal road and take a bus to some town that I had never been to. Sometimes I went with others, sometimes alone. I liked just drifting among the local people, looking at places of historical interest and eating food from street vendors. On one particular day, I traveled up north to the ancient port of Acre. It is one of the oldest continuously inhabited settlements on Earth and was an important city during the Crusades. I spent a full day just walking around in this historical goldmine. I devoured delicious falafel from a street vendor and then caught the bus heading back down the coast to the kibbutz.

I was in a dreamy state after a satisfying day of exploring the port of Acre when I noticed, sitting across the aisle from me a few rows back, an attractive young woman. She had light brown hair and was wearing a summer dress. She seemed to have almost translucent blue eyes. I couldn't look away as much as I tried, not wanting to make her uncomfortable. She struck me as European, but I didn't really know. Then I noticed her looking back at me in a friendly and almost inviting way. We exchanged these muted glances for almost an hour. It felt magical. I had just spent the day wandering out in the sun in some ancient city and suddenly found myself staring at an angel. It never occurred to me to get up and approach her since all the seats around her were taken. I just sat there in this daze of infatuation until the bus came to a sudden halt.

This was my stop, so I stood up and headed to the exit. I stood on the side of the coastal highway, glancing back at this intoxicating woman one last time as the bus pulled away. I got this melancholy feeling that comes after a missed opportunity.

I have seen these super aggressive Israeli guys zero in on foreign girls without hesitation. It's like a numbers game for them—rejection does not phase them. I should have spoken to this beautiful woman who was seated only ten feet away from me, but that's never been my nature. I guess I'm just too laid back. I trudged back up the path to Maagan Michael feeling both peaceful and sad at the same time.

Shabbat (which means the Sabbath) is a special time even though this kibbutz was a totally secular community. On Friday nights, people got dressed up a little more than usual, but generally, life there was very casual. The normal summer attire for both men and women was shorts, T-shirts, and sandals, and many people went barefoot. But on Shabbat, the men wore pants and white shirts, although generally not tucked in. The women there were conscious of fashion even if it didn't dominate their lives the way it does in America. They might wear a new blouse or skirt that they bought from the local store or on a trip to Tel Aviv. The dining room tables would have tablecloths on them, and the meal would be boiled chicken with potatoes and vegetables. There was often an evening program afterward, featuring a concert or a movie in the auditorium. Later on, there was a discotheque for the younger crowd. It was a nice change of pace from the heavy emphasis placed on work throughout the week.

On the Friday evening following my trip to Acre, I put on my white shirt and jeans and headed up to the dining hall. It was a warm summer night on the Mediterranean coast, and the air smelled sweet. I walked into the entrance, where all the people happily exchanged greetings of "Shabbat Shalom, Shabbat Shalom." I wasn't sure who I might eat with, so I looked around to see where some of my friends were seated. It was a very family-oriented place, but since I had no family there, I was kind of a free agent. I scanned the room, and my gaze suddenly became fixated on a table in the back.

Was that the girl I'd seen the other day on the bus? No way. That didn't make any sense. I did a double take and then moved closer. It was her!

She was sitting with a woman from the kibbutz, and I was stunned. Sometimes when something occurs that is so out of context, you struggle to wrap your brain around it. Like a magnet, I was pulled toward her. There was an empty seat at their table, so I asked if they minded if I joined them. They graciously said, "Please do." As I sat down, the woman from the kibbutz stood up and said, "Excuse me. I'll be right back."

That was strange. Now it was just the two of us. I sat there for a moment and then said, "I saw you on the bus from Acre a couple of days ago, correct?"

"Yes. I recognize you too," she replied in English with a cultured accent.

I said, "I'm surprised to see you here." At this point, I was totally blown away but I just tried to maintain my cool.

"Yes, I'm visiting my friend who just left."

"Oh, that's great. My name is Charles."

"I'm Sybille."

"Where are you from?" I asked. Our eyes were locked as these little questions just flowed one after another.

"France. And you?"

"I'm from New Jersey." We both seemed to be leaning forward as we were speaking.

I asked her, "Have you eaten already?"

"No," she replied.

"Should we go up and get some food, or would you rather wait for your friend?"

"I don't know when she'll be coming back. Now is good."

So we walked up together to the buffet. We sat and ate, making light conversation about where we were from and things like that. She told me she was twenty-three, and I said that I was twenty-eight. She was even more beautiful than when I'd seen her on the bus. We finished, and I ask her what she was going to do next.

She said, "I don't know. What would you like to do?"

I said, "We can take a walk. It's a nice night."

So we walked down the path overlooking the sea, enjoying the air, fragrant with the flowers from the grapefruit orchards mixing with the salty air. Suddenly and almost naturally, she took my hand. I thought I was in heaven. *How is this happening?*

Then we stopped. I said, "There's my room. Would you like to come in? I could make us some tea." Maybe subconsciously I had led her to my room. Whereas on the bus, I'd frozen up and couldn't speak to her, now I felt emboldened, as if this were meant to be.

She replied, "I would love that."

We entered, and she sat on the edge of my bed while I went to the hot plate and put the water on for tea. She asked if I could play her a song, pointing to my guitar leaned against the wall in the corner. I handed her the tea and sat down opposite her on a chair, then strummed some mellow chords and fell into a song that I had written years before. It's a quiet song, and I was singing in my low, gravelly voice. At the last chord and with eyes closed, I let it resonate until it was gone. I opened my eyes and found Sybille smiling at me adoringly.

She said, "That was beautiful. Come sit next to me."

I had noticed this exquisite woman several days ago and many miles from here but never said a word to her. Now she was sitting next to me on my bed! We looked into each other's eyes. Hers were pale blue, and mine are dark brown. Her skin was fair, while mine was deeply tanned. Her hair was light and wavy with traces of blonde and brown. Mine was long and curly and bleached out by the sun, while my beard was dark. It was as if we were from two different tribes but somehow had found each other.

We slowly began to kiss. The sweetness, the tenderness, the wonder, all flowed from the surreal circumstances of how we'd met. We got undressed, and her soft white skin was pressed against my hard dark body. Every feature about her was magnificent. Her face, skin, breasts, legs, everything. We were taking our time with every kiss and caress. She was breathing harder and harder, and I slowly began to enter her when she said, "Be gentle, this is my first time." This blew my mind. She was a virgin? My head was spinning.

We stayed lost in each other's eyes the whole time. She really was like an angel. Every nuanced expression on her face, every sound she made, reverberated deep in my soul. Slow, and then fast, and then a little faster, and then slow again, and then barely moving at all, we were fully immersed in this expression of true romance—excitement, pleasure, pain, and joy. We climaxed together in a state of ecstasy unlike any other I've ever known. We lingered in the afterglow, and then began again. I felt like I'd received a gift from the universe for reasons I'd never understand.

After several hours, I got up and made us some more tea. As we sat up and drank, Sybille told me that she was leaving for France the next afternoon. Somehow this seemed to fit with everything else that had occurred. She wrote down her address for me to write her. She needed to stay the night at her friend's apartment and pack in the morning, so we got dressed and walked to her friend's place. She told me what time her bus would be leaving for the airport, then we kissed and said goodnight. I slowly made my way back in the darkness as if in a dream.

The next day was Saturday, a day of rest, and I woke up in a state of wonderment. *Did that really happen?* I washed up and made my way to the dining hall. Sitting alone, I sipped some coffee and ate some toast. Glancing at my watch and seeing that it was almost time for Sybille's bus to arrive out on the Coast Road, I walked to the bus stop and found her standing there with her suitcases. We held hands and just stood in the sunlight waiting for the bus to arrive. We didn't speak much. When the bus came rumbling up and screeched to a halt, we looked at each other and kissed. Without saying a word, she climbed in, and I watched the bus pull away.

Life goes on, but I still treasure this memory of a strange but beautiful gift bestowed on me out of nowhere. Over time, Sybille and I exchanged some letters from her home in France. She wrote that she was now attending nursing school in some place called Lille. There was talk of me coming to France to visit her, but I never did. Instead, I remained in the comfort of the life I had established in Israel. I've always carried some regret in my heart that I chose to stay rather than to go.

When I first saw Sybille on that bus from Acre, I didn't speak up, and immediately it felt like a missed opportunity. The concept of missed opportunities is something everyone is familiar with. That feeling of "what might've been" unifies the human race in varying degrees of regret. Deep thinkers obsess about imaginary paths never taken. Shallow thinkers consider it a waste of time. I'm not sure which perspective is more desirable, but I know where I land—it's in the deep end of the pool. Ultimately, you are who you are. As time goes on, I keep adding new entries to my list of missed opportunities.

During my three years in Israel, I worked hard, got strong in mind and body, learned a new language, made love to some exotic women from foreign lands, and visited places I'd only read about in books. I broadened my knowledge of myself, my heritage, and the world around me. If I could time travel to any period in my life, I would probably choose that one above all others. I often felt part of something greater than myself. At other times, I was as lonely as I have ever been in my life. Israel is a magical and complex place—so much history, so many cultures, so many conflicts. Experiencing it in person opened my eyes to the diverse influences colliding and yet coexisting in this small sliver of land created out of horror and triumph.

And then the time came for me to choose. Would I become a citizen of Israel, adopt Hebrew as my primary language, join the Israeli Defense Force, and make a commitment to a country that I hadn't been born in? Or would I embrace these three years as a "once in a lifetime" experience and simply go back home? This was a difficult and consequential decision.

I ultimately decided to return to America and begin the next chapter of my life. I was thirty years old. My time in the Holy Land had infused me with health and strength and confidence. Those blessings would stay with me forever. I had gained a broader understanding of myself and respect for the diversity of others. I would apply these newly acquired assets as I sought my place in the New World. I had no plan in place, but what else was new? I was ready to dive into the next adventure head first, while hoping the water wasn't too shallow.

CHAPTER FIVE

PARADISE LOST

BEING HOME IN NEW JERSEY was a culture shock. Driving around on roads that had been familiar to me now felt surreal. I had been part of a community in Israel, and now I was a total free agent. I could go anywhere at any time and do anything I wanted. Of course, I had almost no money, so that was a problem. I immediately got a job as a construction laborer and fell right into line carrying heavy stuff for relatively low pay. Did I have any ambition at all? Was my education a complete waste of time and money? Unbeknownst to me, my father had borrowed the money for my college education. My parents had been paying back the loan, but after my father died my mother just stopped making the payments. I only found out about it after I returned from Israel. Now I was responsible for paying it back with exorbitant interest to boot.

I pushed a lot of wheelbarrows and carried a lot of lumber to settle that debt, which took several years to resolve.

In spite of these financial woes, I was actually in a pretty good state of mind. I was thirty years old and probably in the best shape of my life. I had spent the last three years working my ass off with tough Israelis on the Mediterranean coast. I was strong both mentally and physically. I exuded an aura of health and confidence and felt ready for whatever awaited me on the next stop of my journey.

After a few months of living at home and working as a laborer, I had put a little money together. I decided to drive to Upstate New York to visit some old friends from my days at the University of Virginia. I had been going up to Saratoga Springs, a beautiful, historical town nestled in the Adirondack Mountains, for years. I was graciously invited to stay for as long as I wanted by Rocky and Cheryl, a nice couple I'd known for many years. They had a house out in the woods on the shores of Lake Lonely. Rocky was a carpenter, and I soon began working with him. Cheryl had a job as a surveyor. In the evening after dinner, the three of us would sit around the fireplace drinking beer and playing guitar. They were mellow people living in a mellow place. I fit right in.

Over time, I unexpectedly found myself becoming attracted to Cheryl. I had always liked her, but especially now that I was around her every day. She was not some classic beauty, but there was something about her that moved me. She had long, flowing black hair, piercing brown eyes, and a shapely figure. But beyond the physical, I think it was her personality that drew me to her. She was down-to-earth, intelligent, humorous, and a genuinely good person. She might've hailed from a Jewish family on Long Island, but she was no Jewish American princess. Far from it.

Rocky was a nice guy and my friend, and I did not want to fuck that up. I had done that once before down in Kentucky. But I couldn't help noticing that he seemed to take Cheryl for granted. This often happens with couples who have been living together for a long time. Whenever Rocky and I were in town, he always had a roving eye toward any attractive female passing by. He would occasionally complain about being tied down to one woman. That's not so unusual. And so what if I had feelings for his woman who I saw every day? That was also natural and not problematic just so long as I kept it in check. I obviously did not share any of this with our other friends in town. They would've certainly chastised me for rocking the boat of their peaceful little community.

When I realized I simply could not put the brakes on my growing affection for Cheryl, it occurred to me that I should leave this place and go back to New Jersey. But then one night after our guitar jam, I felt compelled to express my feelings. Sitting there with Rocky and Cheryl, I suddenly blurted out that I was falling in love with her. I thought I was just being honest, but it was impulsive and probably a stupid thing to do.

Rocky replied, not to me but to Cheryl, "What do you think about what our charming friend just said?"

She said, "I can't say anything." She then went upstairs, and Rocky and I continued jamming as if nothing had happened.

Days went by as Rocky and I kept working together. We never mentioned my spontaneous outburst again. However, something had changed between Cheryl and me. I could now feel the sexual magnetism in the air, yet we kept our distance so as not to do anything foolish. I guess my dumb proclamation of love had planted a seed in her. Was I a creep for interfering with them or was I there for some greater purpose? I certainly hadn't planned any of it.

One evening, the three of us were going into town. Rocky drove, I sat up front, and Cheryl sat behind me. Suddenly I felt her hand reach around the seat by the passenger door and secretly start stroking my arm. It was only for a minute, but I felt we were now headed either toward disaster or paradise. On another night after work, I was taking a shower, and the bathroom door opened and Cheryl slipped in. Rocky was on the phone, and I guess she wanted to be alone with me if even just for a moment. This was getting dangerous.

One day Rocky had no work for me, so I stayed at the house and helped Cheryl with some chores. We were stacking firewood in the backyard. While passing by each other, I impulsively reached out and pulled her into my arms. I could feel her hugging me back, her hand on my neck. This triggered an emotional response that elevated our relatively innocent flirtation to a whole other level. I was in love, and she might be too.

We decided to go for a ride in her pickup truck to talk about our dilemma. We felt like outlaws because by now the others knew something was up. If this went any further, I would be cast out as a pariah and a homewrecker.

God only knows why, but she made the decision to leave her home on Lake Lonely to go with me. Within the confines of our little universe, this was an earth-shattering event. When I had decided to drive to Upstate New York, I'd never envisioned something like this happening. Later that evening, we sat there and broke the news to Rocky. This required tremendous courage on the part of

Cheryl. I didn't say much. Rocky seemed to take it in stride—no anger, no yelling, no recriminations. Maybe he was relieved to finally gain his freedom. I didn't really know.

We packed up and left two days later, during which time I only hoped Rocky wouldn't kill me in my sleep. I was now hated by my former friends, but I understood this was the price.

Cheryl and I drove away from the shores of Lake Lonely like we were fleeing the scene of a crime. She had packed up her car with her necessary belongings and followed me to my sister's house outside of Boston. We'd had an unspoken agreement that we wouldn't have sex while she was still living with Rocky. I was attempting to be moral in this regard, but there were those who questioned my morality regarding this entire affair anyway. I can understand that, but our destiny superseded the judgment of others. We had overcome great adversity to arrive at this moment. You could say we had our honeymoon in the guest room at my sister's house. I remember that first time we stared into each other's eyes, spoke sweet words, and then kissed and felt each other's bodies. We had built up so much physical and emotional energy in anticipation of this moment. It was a powerful experience that justified all the upheaval we had created along the way.

From Boston, we headed to Woodstock, New York, where we left Cheryl's car at my friend's farm. We then had to pass through another ring of fire. Her parents had demanded that we come to Long Island. They had a few questions.

Cheryl was understandably nervous about facing her parents, who had contributed toward the building of her house in Saratoga. They also were very fond of Rocky, but they wondered why he and Cheryl had never gotten married. After all, they wanted grandchildren! I felt completely calm as we pulled up in front of their ranch house in a Long Island suburban development.

Cheryl hugged her parents and then introduced me. They greeted me with suspicion. After all, I was an interloper and an agent of change. We sat in their wood-paneled den and made small talk while eating snacks her mother had prepared. Then the interrogation began. "How did this happen? What about the house? What about Rocky?" They were upset but not hysterical. When they discovered that I had been living in Israel, the whole dynamic changed. Her father jumped up and put his slides of their trip to Israel on his projector. What began as the Spanish Inquisition had suddenly turned into a nostalgic travelogue.

Her mother finally said, "Herb, turn off the projector. I want to know what your plans are."

I calmly said, "I'm in love with Cheryl, and I want to marry her."

Silence temporarily fell over the room. That was an unrehearsed remark that had just come out of nowhere.

Her mother replied, "What are you going to do when you two have a disagreement?"

Cheryl smiled and responded, "It won't be a problem. We agree on everything."

That naive comment would come back to haunt us later on, but meanwhile, I had passed the interview. They hugged Cheryl and even hugged me. We got back in the car and headed for the Jersey Shore, our next stop on the Magical Mystery Tour.

We spent a few days at my mother's apartment in Asbury Park and went to the beach, out to dinner, and to a movie just like regular people rather than refugees. From there, we embarked on the long trip to Western Kentucky, where we would get a place and find jobs. We were flying blind, but we were young and in love, and we didn't care.

When we finally arrived in Murray, Kentucky, it was the middle of the summer and about 100 degrees. I remember us going into a Kmart just to be inside some air conditioning. Through an old friend, we found a place to rent out in the country. I immediately resumed cutting tobacco, and Cheryl was able to land a part-time job as a surveyor. We'd make dinner at night and then play guitars and go to bed early. She had virtually swapped out her life in Saratoga with Rocky for a similar existence in Kentucky with me, and it went pretty well for a while. She liked country living, and with her pleasing personality, she fit in easily with my friends. She even tried her hand at cutting tobacco on her days off from surveying.

When tobacco season came to an end, I suggested that she and I go to Israel. Finally, we stumbled onto something that we didn't agree on. Cheryl was Jewish, but it was of no importance to her. She felt no connection to Israel. I tried to convince her of the many beautiful aspects of living there, but I couldn't sell it. At the same time, she was getting letters and phone calls from her friends in Saratoga. Apparently, Rocky had fallen into a deep depression as a result of her departure. She was starting to feel guilty and shared her feelings with me. I listened and was sympathetic. This was the beginning of the end. It had been about three months since we'd left Saratoga, and she was getting homesick. In addition, her father had fallen ill, and she felt like she needed to go back home. I understood all her concerns, but I still didn't want her to go. But all of these things taken together sapped the magic out of us.

We packed up and headed back to the Northeast. The ride down had been filled with affection and humor. The ride back was quiet. I dropped her at her car in Woodstock and told her that I wished her father a quick recovery. She said she'd call me when she could. She never did.

I drove back to the Jersey Shore with a heavy heart. When you have such strong conviction that something is right, it is crushing when you discover that you were wrong.

I found a new apartment and a job working construction. I kept hoping to hear from Cheryl, but how would she even reach me? This was before cell phones. After I got my bearings, I called her parents and her mother answered. I asked how Herb was, and she said he was recovering from a heart attack, and Cheryl was living back in Saratoga. I gave her mother my address, hoping Cheryl would write me a letter. Weeks later, a letter arrived. It was a long and rambling description of her feelings, her reflection on what happened, and her plans going forward. It was a mix of regret, blame, and heartache. She was staying at a friend's house because Rocky was not making it easy for her, unsure if he could trust her again. She said that in another life she belonged with me, yet she blamed me for seducing her into leaving Rocky. She even compared my power over her to Svengali! That was crazy talk. Placing blame at the feet of others for our own actions is part of human nature. God knows that I've done it myself, but that doesn't make it true, just easier than looking in the mirror.

As bad as I was feeling, I felt even worse for Cheryl and the pain she was going through. We both would feel ripple effects of our ill-fated romance for years to come. Maybe in the end, I was just a vehicle to reunite her and Rocky. I don't really know. I'm not smart enough to fathom things like that. She ended her letter by warning me not to ever come there because Rocky would kill me. That seemed kind of harsh. I actually had been thinking about going there with the intention of winning her back, but I never went. Her letter worked. It was over. My faith in the concept of a soulmate was crushed forever.

CHAPTER SIX

THE JERSEY SHORE

MY BROKEN HEART SLOWLY HEALED, but it took a little longer to regain confidence in my instincts. I had gone all in with those instincts and had taken a beating in the process. Any commitment issues that I may have already had were further exacerbated by this disappointing episode. Nevertheless, I vowed that I would not let this setback destroy me.

I put all that aside and took stock of my current situation. I had spent the past three years living in what was essentially a socialist society on an Israeli kibbutz. Now I suddenly found myself in the real world where, as they say, "Money talks and bullshit walks!" I once read a thought-provoking book entitled *The Secret History of the World*. It described how early man roamed the sparsely populated Earth with the sole purpose of finding food and shelter.

He relied on his Third Eye to steer him along in this nomadic existence. As the world became increasingly more crowded, he lost some of his natural instincts and replaced them with social skills. Bartering became a way of life, which led to the creation of arbitrarily determined articles of value. Those objects became coins, which then became real money. At that point, the world officially changed. The accumulation of riches became the driving force throughout the land and for the rest of time. It took a while, but mankind went from trading pieces of rock to building supercomputers that could transfer wealth at the speed of light.

So what was I doing? I was still pushing rocks around in a wheelbarrow! I could have been the star of that commercial that said, "Even a caveman could do it!" Growing up, everybody always told me, "You're really smart." My results up to this point did not bear that out. But I was still young enough to make my mark, so in 1985 I formed a company that paid other poor slobs to carry rocks and wood and buckets of nails, and I named it DuroCraft Construction.

I took this endeavor seriously and did everything by the book. I was introduced to an accountant, with whom I have remained friends to this day. Russ helped me get a federal tax identification number and set up a monthly payroll tax schedule. I felt like my circuitous journey had finally led me to a place of legitimacy. I purchased business cards and T-shirts stamped with the company motto—*Built to Last.* There was paperwork, payroll, and insurance associated with such an enterprise, and I immersed myself in all of it. All I needed were customers! I was surprisingly aggressive in advertising in the local paper. In fact, I was the first one in the area to ever purchase ads for building residential decks.

This was during a time when decks were very popular, and I quickly gained expertise on constructing these attractive home appendages. The guys I hired were all good carpenters, but they generally possessed some major character flaws such as alcoholism, drug use, or problems with the law. For some reason, my crew at DuroCraft became a magnet for talented degenerates. Miraculously, the work always turned out well.

The business grew, and I took on bigger projects that involved supplying labor to larger established contractors. It was exciting in the sense that the dollar amounts involved were greater, although that proved to be somewhat of an illusion. In retrospect, I really wasn't very smart. I had unwittingly placed myself at the center of the labor market where opposing forces squeezed me from both sides. Owing to the scale of these projects, my payroll had ballooned, which meant that my profits had to balloon as well. My survival depended on this fragile equation. How did I not foresee this happening? I tried to stand my ground, but I could feel the vise closing in on me.

Why couldn't I have just remained in Israel and gotten up early and caught nets of fish and eaten olives and hummus and gone to bed with beautiful women from foreign lands? Instead, I got a late start in a world more complicated and devious than my nature could abide. I would spend the next forty years basically behind the eight ball. The *Never a Break* era had begun!

In my quest to survive in a world where I did not belong, I exhibited perseverance and honesty. The former was a result of the hard physical labor hammered into my bones. The element of honesty was more innate, and I embraced it as the driving principle in my life. In the real world, perseverance may propel you forward, but honesty can actually drag you back. I recognized this unfortunate dichotomy in my efforts to sustain a business but decided that when all accounts were settled, I wanted some recognition of integrity carved into my tombstone. There are paupers' graveyards and fancy mausoleums, but whether you lived rich or poor, either way you end up as dust. I somehow find comfort in that knowledge.

The first time I ever went to Atlantic City was by sheer coincidence. I was visiting my old girlfriend, Lynn, in South Jersey, and her brother-in-law, Jimmy, begged me to drive him to a casino. We landed at the Atlantis, which was formerly the Playboy Club and eventually became Trump Plaza. Years later, it was demolished, with its cursed remains deposited in a local landfill.

As soon as we arrived, Jimmy began drinking heavily. He parked himself at a blackjack table and bought a few hundred dollars in chips. Since the drinks were free, he instructed the cocktail waitress to just keep 'em coming, one Kahlúa and cream after another. I barely knew this guy, and now I was stuck there with some loud, inebriated stranger determined to lose every dollar he had. I had to separate myself from this knucklehead.

This atmosphere was as unappealing and foreign to me as the surface of the moon would be. I wandered around aimlessly until I eventually found myself standing at the end of a crowded craps table. Men and women were hootin' and hollerin' with every toss of the dice. Everybody seemed to be having a good time. I had $500 in my pocket, so I bought some chips and asked the guy next to me what I should I do next. He gave me a brief tutorial on how to play. I immediately started winning money. I guess this was what you would call "a hot table." The dice eventually came to me. I didn't know what I was doing, but the crowd kept cheering and the dealer kept pushing more chips at me. I tossed those bones like an old pro, throwing one number after another. I felt like a hero, if only for twenty minutes or so. On a craps table, that's enough to make you very popular with total strangers. When the dust settled, I had doubled my money.

I looked up and spotted Jimmy approaching on unsteady feet. Slurring his words, he asked, "Can we leave now?" He had lost everything he had.

With some difficulty, we located my car in the mammoth parking garage. We headed for home on the Atlantic City Expressway, and I just hoped he wouldn't throw up in my car. We made it back to the house and regaled the girls with tales of our exploits. They had dinner waiting for us. Lynn and I had lived together down in Kentucky several years earlier, so after dinner, we went up to her room and made love as we had done a hundred times before. It felt natural for us to maintain a physical relationship even though we were no longer a couple. So, I doubled my money and had sex with my former girlfriend. All things being equal, it was a good day.

The following week, I drove to the Monmouth Mall and bought several books about playing craps. I studied them from cover to cover. Then I went back to Atlantic City, and I won again. Combining book learning and real-life experience, I adopted a method of betting that embraced the most favorable odds in the casino. I was not a mathematical genius by any stroke of the imagination. In fact, even though I was in the Honors Math Class in high school, I was probably ranked eleventh out of the twelve nerdy students in the class. However, I was closer to the top in the Honors English Class and graduated seventh in my class out of 250 students overall! Just thought I would mention that. Anyway, my method wasn't exactly a "system," but more of an approach. I read that most gamblers who bragged about the infallibility of their system usually died broke.

I bought another book written by Lyle Stuart called *Casino Gambling for the Winner*. He was a legendary gambler and book publisher. I gleaned one important lesson from that book that I never forgot—quit while you're ahead. I know that sounds simplistic, but its application was quite advanced when developed into a habit. His premise was that at some point during almost every session, you find yourself winning. Ideally, if you just quit then, you would always be a winner. It might be a lot or it might be a little, but you'd be a winner nevertheless. Here is where it got tricky. You would be bucking human nature with its tendencies toward greed and cockeyed optimism. Self-discipline was the only thing standing between you and those destructive tendencies. As my knowledge of the game grew, so did my resolve. I kept a ledger of my results, finding that I won fifteen times in a row by sticking to that advice. Of course, there was the occasional session when I was never ahead. This was problematic because you could blow five winning sessions with one outsized loss by chasing your money. I found that I had a lot more discipline when I was winning than when I was losing. This was a metaphor for some greater life lesson, but I had no idea what that was. I would end up figuring it out later.

In general, my approach worked best when I drove to the casino alone. When with a group or even one other person, the ability to go home to secure a win could be impeded by social obligations. Most people just wanted to keep playing until some mutually agreed upon departure time arrived. They either won or lost depending on where they stood when the music stopped. It's hard to kill hours and hours in a casino just waiting for the other guys to finish. All ventures are fraught with pitfalls either from inner demons or external hazards. I'm not sure which are easier to control.

I gave the Lyle Stuart book to my friend Rich, who also bought into the "hit and run" approach. We drove down together several times and were able to execute the strategy with varying degrees of success. He sometimes wandered from the basic methodology by stretching it beyond its limits. On one occasion in particular, Rich got a little carried away. We had left the craps table with chips in hand. On the way to the cashier, we passed a blackjack table. He noticed an open seat at the very end of the table. This is called "third base," and the decision by that player to take a card or stand pat can determine the outcome for the whole table. Rich impulsively placed all his chips in a disorganized pile on the betting line in front of third base. Seated at the table was a group of five senior citizens placing small bets and passing the time, and now this interloper had barged in and disrupted their peaceful game.

The dealer stared coldly at Rich and asked, "Is that a bet?" He muttered that it was, so the dealer stacked the chips, which came out to some odd number like $173. He began to deal. Some of the players stayed pat with eighteen or nineteen and some took hits and busted out. Rich hit to a twelve and miraculously got a nine for twenty-one! The dealer turned over a sixteen and drew a four for twenty. Everybody else at the table lost except for Rich, and their hatred for him was palpable. The dealer paid him, and he awkwardly gathered up his chips with both hands. As he got up to leave, he accidentally knocked over his neighbor's cocktail with his elbow. The drink spilled all over the table. The dealer had daggers in his eyes as he watched Rich shuffle away. Although he was my closest friend, I edged away from this pariah as I envisioned an angry mob of seniors in walkers and wheelchairs chasing him through the casino.

By now, I was in my mid-thirties and simultaneously juggling a struggling business, a volatile gambling venture, and an active social life. I was single and in my prime. I had money and confidence and seemed to meet women without really trying. Although I went out a lot back then to bars and restaurants, I was never one of those slick guys who thrived in that environment. They had the whole pickup scene wired with smooth talk, good looks, and fancy cologne. It was practically a business for these would-be gigolos.

In contrast, I was just a quiet guy looking for an evening out. I usually stood alone in the back, sipping a Scotch and listening to the band. I occasionally met some women in these establishments, but purely by accident. I also went on numerous blind dates initiated by well-intentioned wives of friends. I had the right attitude for these perilous adventures and was always a gentleman. Working construction, playing craps, and going on blind dates had resulted in a mixed drink of uncertainty that characterized my life during this time.

I tried to offset my nightly routine of going out drinking and eating by working out regularly in a gym. I was steadily gaining weight but didn't realize the extent of it until much later. This life of excess was completely antithetical to the healthy lifestyle of my years living on a kibbutz, and I vowed to change my evil ways before it was too late.

Owning a small construction company was stressful and these diversions helped relieve that stress, but I was determined to make an adjustment in my lifestyle. But before that transformation would take place, I managed to squeeze in a much-needed vacation. My business had slowed down because of the early stages of a recession, so I decided to spend two weeks out west.

I flew into Las Vegas by myself and booked a room at the world-famous Desert Inn. I played craps, ate, drank, and took in the atmosphere of Sin City. I even managed to win a thousand dollars. After three days of debauchery, I rented a car and drove to San Francisco to visit some friends from Israel. After a pleasant weekend with them, I continued my odyssey down the California coast to San Diego, which was 500 miles away. My plan was to return the car rental at the San Diego airport and fly home from there with my prearranged ticket. This was a fairly ambitious itinerary for such a simple man.

I worked my way through Santa Cruz to the old California towns of Monterey and Carmel. I got off the highway to explore some places that John Steinbeck wrote about in *Tortilla Flat* and *Cannery Row*. Monterey had retained its old Spanish flavor, and Carmel was a quaint seaside town whose long-time mayor was none other than Clint Eastwood! I was glad I had taken the time to sample these slices of Americana, but it was getting late. I decided to push on anyway. It was here that I fucked up.

It was dark now as I rose up to the twisting narrow roads overlooking the cliffs of Big Sur. What kind of moron drives through Big Sur at night? Number one, you would miss seeing the incredible beauty of the rugged Los Padre Mountains, which overlooks the crashing waves of the Pacific. Number two, you could get fucking killed! It didn't take long before I reversed my decision to drive on pitch-black roads snaking along the edge of a cliff. Adventurous, yes; suicidal, no. I turned around and carefully worked my way back to the first motel I could find.

After surviving the previous night's idiocy, I awoke to a new day and drove on in full light, marveling at the majesty of Big Sur. I continued on down the coast and exited at San Simeon. This was home of the famous Hearst Castle. Newspaper tycoon William Randolph Hearst began construction of his hilltop mansion in 1919 on the 140,000 acres he'd inherited from his father, George Hearst. George had made his vast fortune in mining before acquiring the *San Francisco Examiner*, the newspaper that became the springboard for his son's future publishing empire.

The Castle was an architectural wonder that took over twenty-five years to fully complete. The materials were brought in from all over the world and hauled up by donkeys to the elevated construction site known as Camp Hill. During the Roaring Twenties, the Hearst Castle was famous for its legendary parties with guests ranging from US presidents to the biggest Hollywood stars of the era. Through his enormous wealth and nationwide newspaper platform, William Randolph Hearst exercised great influence on the American public. His form of "Yellow Journalism" fueled nationalistic fervor marked by racism and anti-immigration sentiment. His views had slowly shifted over time from progressive to isolationist.

Like that of many others, Hearst's business empire was decimated by the Great Depression. The weekend parties ended as massive debt forced the sale of many of his assets. After his death in 1951, the Hearst Castle was ceded to the state of California. It is still a major tourist attraction, with a museum at ground level and sightseeing expeditions of the Castle above. Visitors can ride up in cable cars to reach the top of the hill for lengthy tours of this lavish estate from a bygone era.

I wandered through the museum and marveled at the displays of this period in American history. The early twentieth century has always been of interest to me. I studied the mustachioed faces of these men of consequence in the faded photographs and newsreels. Their expressions were grave and their wardrobes fastidious as they basked in the light of their accomplishments. It struck me as an era of great vanity. I realized that all the people in those photos had been dead for decades. What did it all mean? In a sense, it was like an illusion, as if they'd never existed.

In rare cases, there are monuments like the Hearst Castle serving as a testament to the magnitude of one man's influence. And the wealth amassed by some captains of industry has ended up in philanthropic foundations bearing their names. But not all family fortunes survive, as some have been passed down to generations of bumbling idiots who squabbled over every portion until there was nothing left.

Hearst and his legacy were memorialized in Orson Welles' 1941 iconic film, *Citizen Kane*. Charles Foster Kane's story was loosely based on Hearst's life, while the fictional castle of the movie was called *Xanadu*. Hearst employed every tool at his disposal to stop its release, but he ultimately failed. *Citizen Kane* went on to be ranked by the American Film Institute as the number one film of all time.

For some unknown reason, I did not take the tour up to the top of Camp Hill. Maybe there wasn't one scheduled that afternoon, or perhaps I just wanted to get back on the road. I really don't remember. In retrospect, I believe not walking through the halls of the Hearst Castle was just one more missed opportunity.

Instead, I continued down the Pacific Coast Highway, spending the night in a motel in Laguna Beach, south of Los Angeles. I had passed through Laguna before on a summer vacation in college. I loved that place—a classic California beach town with good restaurants, a pristine beach, and beautiful women. The following day, I headed south, stopping at other beach towns like San Juan Capistrano and San Clemente. I arrived in San Diego well ahead of my scheduled flight back to New Jersey.

I got back home and within a few days it was as if I'd never gone away. I guess that's just the transient nature of vacations. I quickly changed gears and recalibrated the current status of DuroCraft. My crew had been off for two weeks and needed to get back to work, so I had to drum up some new business. Keeping them busy and also keeping the money flowing in were unstable elements in this type of business. Slow periods like these caused doubt to creep into my assessment of what I was doing with my life. Nevertheless, I stayed with it for a couple more years, always wondering what was coming next.

CHAPTER SEVEN

THE WANDERING JEW

IN THE BACK OF MY mind, I thought that I had the temperament to succeed as a professional gambler. It was kind of a romantic notion that I could lead an unconventional life like that. Using the Lyle Stuart philosophy, I had been a consistent winner simply by quitting while I was ahead. Self-discipline was now deeply ingrained in me, and my understanding of the game was crystal clear. As it turned out, there were a lot of other aspects to this undertaking that were not yet fully understood.

My company, DuroCraft, had now hit the wall during the recession that straddled the late eighties and early nineties. I didn't have enough work to keep the guys busy, plus the cost of maintaining a business was eating into my savings. I made an executive decision to suspend all company activities without formally terminating DuroCraft. This was a big step.

A job interview was arranged for me by a friend with the largest construction company in the world, Turner Construction. Unfortunately, it was in Tempe, Arizona. I decided to go for it, packed up my Ford Explorer, and headed out West. My destination was 2,000 miles to the southwest, but being the genius that I am, I proceeded first to drive 300 miles to the Northeast to visit my sister on Cape Cod. Afterward, I planned to pass through the Great Lakes region before heading south. It was an exciting journey into the unknown, and I had undertaken such expeditions before, having blindly moved to both Kentucky and Israel.

There was some element in my psyche that was amenable to living one step at a time, and I sincerely believe that I became a better man because of those experiences. It's kind of funny that all these decades later I'm still living one step at a time. Everybody is different, and in the end, you are who you are.

Everything I needed was loaded into my truck on the outside chance that I would get the job and actually make a life for myself out West. I was like a modern version of those Okies in *The Grapes of Wrath* heading out to California to pick oranges and melons. The difference was that I wasn't lumbering along in a broken-down jalopy filled to the brim with furniture, clothes, and ragged kids or escaping the hardships of the Depression. I was just taking a shot at something new.

I had two weeks before my interview, so I took my time, averaging about 500 miles a day. I didn't exactly have a fixed route planned for this trip, figuring I would just wing it—an approach that had both pluses and minuses attached to it. Excitement and confusion would be the simplest way of defining those opposing forces. I worked my way from Massachusetts into New York, where I hit Lake Ontario and Niagara Falls, then down to Lake Erie where I impulsively jumped on Interstate 75 that heads due south through Ohio and Kentucky. This was my first trip cross-country in a number of years, and my senses were reawakened to just how big this country is. A torrential rainfall hit in Kentucky, and I could barely see ten feet in front of me as tractor trailers were whizzing by undeterred. Forced off the road, I found some fleabag motel for the night.

The next day, I devoured a country breakfast of eggs, grits, and biscuits and gravy before finding my way to Interstate 40 West. The greatest sight I saw was when I crossed over the Mississippi River on the bridge leaving Memphis, Tennessee, and landing in West Memphis, Arkansas. The view of the river was so mind-boggling that I turned around and crossed it again. That iconic river starts as a trickle out of a lake in northern Minnesota and gains strength as it cuts through the country before pouring into the Gulf of Mexico south of New Orleans. The width and power of the Mississippi has long been a towering presence as a creator of natural borders and an irreplaceable avenue of commerce. It's also been a source of devastating floods, periodically wiping out small towns clinging perilously to its banks. As just a guy crossing a bridge, I could feel Mark Twain's *Life on the Mississippi* come alive in my imagination, and I savored this moment.

I got off the interstate and made my way through the Ozark Mountains, witnessing a hard-scrabble reality far removed from my upbringing on the Jersey Shore. The people just looked different, and their shacks and country stores reminded me of the poverty so prevalent in rural America.

I ultimately reached Oklahoma, where the topography dramatically changed to stark desert plains and large stone formations. Everything went from lush green forests to sand colored hues of rock and dust. I pushed on to the Texas Panhandle and saw road stands of Indians selling turquoise trinkets. There was a big billboard outside Amarillo that advertised a seventy-two-ounce T-bone steak you could get for free if you could finish it. To me, Texas felt almost like another planet in the solar system.

By the time Texas turned into New Mexico, I was getting tired. I had already been on the road for about five days. Finally, I crossed into Arizona with its cartoonish green cactus extruding out of the sandy ground and then arrived in Scottsdale, just outside of Phoenix. I would be staying with my brother-in-law's mother. It was summer and 110 degrees outside. People kept saying, "But it's a dry heat!" Even the pool was too hot to swim in. All I could think was, *What if I actually land this job and have to move here?*

On the day of my big interview, I put on the one suit I owned with a flashy paisley tie and polished my only pair of dress shoes. I was ready and brimming with confidence. I arrived outside Turner's offices in my dusty Ford Explorer loaded with all my possessions. I met with a manager and presented my resume. He read it, all the while glancing at me, then asked, "Are you familiar with the standardized job estimating software for hi-rise construction?"

Come again? I thought to myself. I could try to bluff my way through this or simply admit that I didn't even own a computer. My experience was building shit in the field and running herd over a crew of misfits who ultimately got the job done right. I didn't know how to communicate that in language that would resonate with such a corporate stiff. I quickly opted for the middle ground, stressing my hands-on experience and natural-born talent as a fast learner. I chose not to mention that I graduated seventh in my class in high school, but this guy kept going back to the technology stuff. I couldn't help wondering if this was just the luck of the draw that I got this particular interviewer. I was like a fish out of water trying to impress a gatekeeper who held my fate in his hands. I might as well have told him how many pushups I could do. I was used to swinging a hammer but I felt like I was applying for a job as a nuclear physicist.

"I'm sorry, Mr. Levinsohn, but you're not what we're looking for here at Turner Construction. Thank you for coming in."

I thought to myself, *Coming in? What the fuck? I just drove 2,000 miles!* Then I shuffled off to my truck and immediately ripped that stupid tie off from around my neck.

The funny thing is that had I talked my way into that company, I might have stayed there for my entire career. Anyone with any ability who simply showed up every day would organically move up the food chain. In the end, every executive at Turner Construction retires as a multimillionaire. Well, at least I gave it the old college try—nothing ventured, nothing gained. I have often taken comfort in little clichés like that.

I picked myself up and with guarded optimism moved on to my next destination—Las Vegas! I had gone out there ten years earlier on a weeklong vacation. As I drove along, I thought about the last time I had visited my hometown poker game before embarking on this latest adventure. I had been playing in that game with the same guys for twenty years. At the end of that night, everyone shook hands with me and wished me luck on my big trip. Big Tony, Lucky, Nino, Kenny the Rake, the House Man, they all extended their well-wishes. The last one was Steve Pizza. This guy lacked a certain wiring that provides normal people with a filter between brain and mouth. In other words, he just said shit. Steve stuck his hand out and said, "You won't make it 'til Christmas." It was just after Labor Day, and this cocksucker was predicting my demise in less than four months! As it turned out, I didn't last until Columbus Day. How that unfolded shall be revealed later, but suffice it to say that every Columbus Day I get a call from Steve reminding me about that fucked-up prediction of his.

So there I was, back on the road, cruising through the Southwest, and despite my failed job interview, I was somehow in a good mood. The air felt warm against my skin, and the rugged terrain looked beautiful and strange. I shot up to Flagstaff and then headed west to Kingman and up through Boulder City to Henderson, Nevada. Soon thereafter, the vibrations began to change as I crossed the Clark County line. Excitement was in the air! When you pass the famous neon sign of Vegas Vic, you have officially crossed the Rubicon into another dimension.

I had been coasting along, breathing in the dry air of the high desert, when suddenly I was immersed in a discombobulated mélange of hotels, billboards, and bumper-to-bumper traffic. The sidewalks were teeming with a sea of humanity oozing greed and desire. Soon enough, I would be among the fish in that sea, driven by questionable impulses and half-baked hopes and dreams.

CHAPTER EIGHT

VIVA LAS VEGAS

My senses were on full alert as I motored down the Las Vegas Strip. I was like some prairie dog with my nose in the air, sniffing out new terrain. The Strip was lined with iconic casino hotels—The Flamingo, The Sands, The Desert Inn, and The Riviera. These older hotels were remnants of the gangster era and the shadowy legends surrounding them. I've read the books and watched the movies and almost wish I had lived back then. Sin City was built on the backs of mob-controlled loans from the Teamster's pension fund. Bribery, crime, and corruption were the tools that got the job done. Organized crime figures from Cleveland, Detroit, Chicago, and New York flocked to the Wild West to make a fresh start. Over time, that dark birthright has been rehabilitated into nostalgia as soulless corporations now reap the rewards of Bugsy Siegel's dream.

So, in the midst of all this colorful history, I arrived on the scene as one man seeking his place in possibly the most corrupt environment on Earth, thinking I could make a go of it there. It was a romantic vision or more likely a romantic delusion. Was I really that special that I could pull this off? Many have tried, and many have been sent packing. They slink home with their tail between their legs, bereft of their savings and their pride. But I did not believe that was going to happen to me. I possessed the winning combination of knowledge, experience, and discipline. Now all I needed was the one most elusive element—luck.

Somehow a journey that started in New Jersey and zigzagged across the entire country had led me to the garish entrance of the Imperial Palace Hotel and Casino. This was a backwater establishment located several blocks off the Strip. It was not exactly a dump, but it was old and lacked the flash that would attract more well-heeled visitors. In fact, it was one of many places in Las Vegas that catered almost exclusively to locals. With its threadbare carpets and worn-out dealers, it offered low stakes blackjack and craps along with the standard all-you-can-eat buffet. Wednesday night was Prime Rib Night for only $5.99!

The primary attraction was the reasonable long-term rate for a hotel room. My loosely conceived plan was that I would stay there for a week or two until I settled into the lifestyle of a professional Vegas gambler. By then, I would have made useful contacts among all the friendly people, and they would be more than willing to help an outsider just arriving in town from Jersey. What the hell was I thinking? This was a community in the sense that a school of sharks is a community. It was survival of the fittest, and nobody was getting any breaks. If you paid your dues and trusted no one, maybe you'd learn the ropes before you went broke. Could I get my bearings and pass through the initial ring of fire? I was a forty-two-year-old man who somehow chose this place to make my stand.

It's true that my experience had been limited to friendly poker games and day trips to Atlantic City. Yes, I had read Lyle Stuart's book from cover to cover and knew what it took to be a winner. I had a modest bankroll and a wealth of confidence built up by years of physical labor. I was strong, relatively good-looking, and raised with solid family values. I was almost too wholesome to find myself in a place crawling with degenerates, prostitutes, gangsters, and thieves. But I was intrigued by the dark side of life rather than intimidated by it. I faced each day in this world of shadows with a bright optimism that could not be crushed.

Every morning I sauntered down to the breakfast buffet on the ground floor of the hotel. I love a breakfast buffet. I like the freedom of movement, the process of selection, the visual attraction of the trays of scrambled eggs, bacon, French toast, bagels, and pastries. The friendly waitress brings me a carafe of coffee and a large orange juice. Life is good—I was a hungry man in the right place. I learned that the key to buffet eating is that if you don't like something, then just don't finish it. The "clean your plate" philosophy we grew up with does not apply. Waste is built into the equation so there's no sense worrying about it. The starving children of Biafra will not benefit whether I finish my corn muffin or not. In a perfect world, that surplus food could be magically transported to those hungry mouths. But if it was a perfect world, they wouldn't be starving in the first place. I ate slowly and read the local paper and tried not to get too stuffed. That can make you stupid, and I would need my wits about me as I faced a new day in Sin City.

Fueled up for what lay ahead, I was moving slowly as I hit the teeming sidewalks. It was already almost 100 degrees. Like at the buffet, I had many choices. I could put on my bathing suit and cool off at the hotel pool. There was always an abundance of bathing beauties at these facilities, providing a welcome distraction from the chaos inside.

Or I could play in an afternoon poker tournament, although I'd been trying to resist the temptation of daytime gambling. Maybe I'd just kill some time and stroll down the Las Vegas Strip. There was a lot to see. The architecture of the hotels fascinated me. I marveled at the imagination and attention to detail that went into the planning of these pleasure palaces. Treasure Island, New York New York, Excalibur, and Mandalay Bay must've been dream projects for any architectural firm to design.

On occasion, I'd get into my Ford Explorer and drive to one of the nearby natural attractions. Lake Mead and the Hoover Dam offered temporary relief from the unyielding stimuli back in town. Just the constant din from the bells and whistles of the slot machines was enough to make you run for the hills. Japanese guards from World War II might've pumped that sound into the cells of POWs to induce sleep deprivation and moral despair.

Red Rock Canyon is ten miles outside of Las Vegas and is like an oasis that has remained untouched by human infiltration. I would drive there just to clear my head. As the sunlight shimmered on the ancient rock formations there, I felt transported to some other time and place. Years later, I drove out there only to discover Red Rock Canyon Hotel and Casino. What a surprise. They even fucked that up!

So there I was, exercising restraint in the gambling capital of the world. I limited myself to only craps and poker, which were my two most proficient games. I didn't play blackjack, slots, or roulette, or go to the Sports Books, even though back home I routinely bet on football games with illegal bookies. Everybody did. It was just part of the fabric of life in Jersey.

I'd brought my infamous notebook with me to record all my results, and my first few entries were not encouraging. As I mentioned before, the only fallacy in my betting philosophy was tied to those sessions when I was never ahead. Then I couldn't lock up even a modest win for the day. That seemed to be happening far too often since I'd arrived and was not a good omen. I kept reminding myself of the gambler's credo, "It's bad luck to be superstitious!" There are so many levels of irony to that statement that Yogi Berra might've authored it!

I walked down to the Desert Inn, one of the oldest resorts on the Strip, built in the 1950s. I stayed there many years ago on my very first Vegas vacation. It was started by a developer named Wilbur Clark but taken over by Moe Dalitz, a transplanted Jewish bootlegger from Cleveland. Moe was formerly affiliated with the notorious Mayfield Road Gang, which controlled the rackets in Cleveland for decades. The Desert Inn, or DI as it was known, was a hugely successful and respected enterprise. Over time, Moe's reputation as an organized crime figure was sanitized by his philanthropic work, and he was once even honored as Las Vegas Man of the Year!

On Thanksgiving of 1966, Moe rented out the top two floors to Howard Hughes for a ten-day stay. When the ten days passed, Moe asked Howard to vacate the premises because those suites had been booked for some high rollers for New Year's Eve. But Howard was in a reclusive state and refused to leave. Moe was reluctant to physically remove one of the richest men in the world, so rather than move out, Howard Hughes bought the place. He stayed at the Desert Inn for four years and never left his bedroom. In fact, he wouldn't even let the hotel staff clean his room. He conducted all his business affairs from that one room, purchasing several other casinos on the Strip. He saw no one. Due to his failing health, he was removed by stretcher in 1970 and flown to the Bahamas. Howard Hughes died in 1976, leaving a legacy as one of the most mysterious figures in American history.

The Desert Inn was designed to be a high-class country club for Hollywood stars and studio executives. Frank Sinatra made his very first appearance in Las Vegas at the DI. It was the only hotel that had enough land to accommodate an eighteen-hole golf course. The atmosphere was sedate, with high-end restaurants and dealers in tuxedos. From the plush carpeting to the cherrywood moldings, opulence oozed out of every corner. Not a place that I would exactly fit in, but the only time I ever played there, I won a lot of money. So, in jeans and a T-shirt, I stepped up to the craps table and tried to reverse the negative trend of my new career. It's strange to think that only a decade before, I had been standing waist-deep in water by the Mediterranean Sea, lifting nets filled with fish. Now I was standing among a crowd of strangers, waving a pair of dice, hoping to toss a winning number. I once lived in the Holy Land and was now standing in possibly the unholiest place on Earth! How I had gotten from Israel to Vegas was a mystery beyond comprehension.

I was getting worn down by my lack of success. I always said that gambling is only fun when you win. Plus, I was starting to feel very lonely. I remember being lonely toward the end of my time in Israel as well. But that was different—I was surrounded by people I knew in a large family-based community. I was personally without family there, and during holidays I felt my isolation more deeply. Although accepted by most, I remained an outsider. In the end, everyone walks through this life alone, but without family, you tend to feel it more acutely.

My Vegas experience was even worse for me in that regard. It was more of an existential loneliness. There were crowds of people and action everywhere, but I didn't know anybody. My personality was not conducive to breaking into some preexisting clique. I might engage in some conversation at a poker table, but that would be the extent of it. Making new friends in your forties is a difficult enough undertaking in a normal environment, but in a place like this, it was nearly impossible. I fell into the routine of the breakfast buffet, followed by a walk, a swim, and then a late afternoon gambling session. Poker and craps, poker and craps, poker and craps—my ledger looked pathetic with so many minus signs preceding growing dollar amounts. I hadn't even been there for a month, but I had to escape with my sanity intact along with what remained of my bankroll. Unlike Howard Hughes, I was not carried out on a stretcher, but I checked out of the Imperial Palace under my own power and headed out of town. It was early October, just before Columbus Day—a date that would live in infamy!

CHAPTER NINE

CALIFORNIA DREAMIN'

I HAULED ASS OUT OF LAS Vegas like I was driving the getaway car for a bank robbery gone bad. Heading south on Highway 15, I crossed the state line into California and continued through the arid Western Desert toward Barstow and Victorville. I could finally breathe again and felt fortunate to have gotten out of Vegas alive. I just needed a little time to fully recover from this latest fiasco. Of course, half my bankroll was gone, but I wasn't complaining. As Kenny Rogers once sang, "You gotta know when to hold 'em and know when to fold 'em." I folded, cashed in my chips, and lived to fight another day. It wasn't the end of the world.

I cut across to Pasadena and then battled through the dense congestion of Greater Los Angeles. My coast-to-coast journey was now finally complete as I parked my dusty Ford Explorer and walked out onto the Santa Monica Pier. I looked out over the Pacific Ocean and breathed in the salty sea air. A cool breeze washed over me, and I felt peaceful for the first time in a month. I may have been 3,000 miles from New Jersey, but the familiarity of sand and sea felt like home. The Pacific is much bluer than the Atlantic. They say it's because of the higher salt content in the water. It looked beautiful to me. I felt revived and put all that had happened to me in the rearview mirror. And I don't just mean what happened to me on this trip—I mean in my whole life! How many fresh starts can one person get? Maybe it's infinite, but that's a question above my pay grade.

Not wanting to trade one urban nightmare for another, I left Santa Monica and drove south on the famous Pacific Coast Highway, also known as the PCH. As I drove along, I flashed back to the first time I'd ever traveled on the PCH. It was back in the early '70s during summer vacation from college when I had hitchhiked cross-country with Carol, whom I had met earlier on Spring Break in Fort Lauderdale. It was not uncommon to do stuff like that back then. I've always wondered what my parents were thinking when I informed them of that half-baked plan. They didn't say it out loud, but it might've been, "Whatever happened to law school?" Or more likely, "Are you out of your mind?" I think they'd already surrendered to the fact that the world had changed and their son, who once possessed so much promise, was now traveling a road not found on any map in their glove compartment. Parents don't give up on their kids easily unless pushed to the absolute limit. I may have disappointed them, but we never became estranged despite whatever heartache I may have caused them.

Those carefree days of college were long gone, but here I was back on the PCH once again. My immediate destination was Laguna Beach, roughly fifty miles south of LA. I planned to check into a motel and stay there until I regained my equilibrium. I was still decompressing from my failed experiment as a professional gambler. Laguna Beach is the perfect place to do just that—beautiful beaches, beautiful women, and tranquil sidewalk cafés. A couple of days of sun and sand and some good Mexican food, and I'd be a new man.

Afterward, I'd continue down the coast to San Diego. Maybe I'd try to make a go of it there. So, let's see—struck out in Arizona, struck out in Las Vegas, and now taking a shot in San Diego. It was a miracle that I was still such an optimist.

With that ancient history behind me, I once again sought relief on the sunny beaches of Southern California. I had fond recollections of the previous times I'd spent in Laguna Beach. Maybe that's why I was so emotionally crushed years later by the raging forest fires that plagued the hills above Laguna. Watching those disasters unfold on my TV from New Jersey, it seemed like the whole state of California was on fire. Exhausted firemen from all over the country worked triple shifts trying to contain this soulless menace. The El Niño winds and weather conspired to impede their progress. The destruction of homes and forests was un-imaginable. I watched one fire creeping toward the Getty Ranch outside of Los Angeles. That's where the priceless art collection of John Paul Getty was housed. Fortunately, the fire didn't make it that far.

As a Jersey guy, I found many aspects of Southern California very appealing. The coastline is much different there with the ocean to the west and mountains to the east. With the Pacific Coast Highway running north and south, it was easy to jump off at any point and explore cool beach towns like Carlsbad, Encinitas, Solana Beach, and Del Mar.

The Mexican food is another thing that I hold in high regard in SoCal. Because of its proximity to the border, there is an abundance of authentic Mexican cuisine ranging from fancy restaurants to inexpensive chains, such as Alberto's and Rubio's Fish Tacos. These chains do not serve crap like Taco Bell—this is real food made by real people.

In New Jersey, the equivalent of this would be the preponderance of pizzerias. Italians are to New Jersey like Mexicans are to Southern California, although my Italian friends would probably get pissed off at that comparison! It's true that Hispanics haven't fully assimilated into American society like European immigrants did during the early twentieth century. That was the era of the Great Melting Pot when people flooded into this country from all over the world. My own great-grandfather, Abraham Levinsohn, emigrated from Russia in 1893. He arrived at Ellis Island and then settled on the Jersey Shore in the town of Belmar.

I may be Jewish, but I grew up on Italian food. Every Sunday night, my family went out for dinner at Freda's Ristorante and Pizzeria on Ridge Avenue in Asbury Park. Antipasto, pizza, and spaghetti and meatballs, followed by Italian pastries, were all served family-style. I can still picture it like it was yesterday. I wish I could experience now what food tasted like back then, but Freda's closed down decades ago after Asbury was decimated by race riots.

Memories of food from when you were young, like music, stay with you for the rest of your life. I'm sure there's some scientific reason for that phenomenon, but I'm no scientist. I'm a writer, a poet, an adventurer, and a dreamer, but definitely not a scientist. Seventh in my class overall in high school, but last in my class in science. The nerdy kids loved experiments in chemistry class, you know, working with all those elements and shit. I did not. Was I too cool for science? That might possibly be the dumbest thing I have ever said.

But you didn't have to be a chemist to remember how good those charcoal burgers tasted fresh off the grill at Max Embers in Long Branch. Or the corned beef sandwiches on rye with mustard from Grossman's Delicatessen in Asbury Park. Or the Chinese barbecued spareribs from Little Szechuan in Little Silver. Food never tasted better than it did back then.

At home on summer nights when our maid was off, my father was in charge of the backyard grill. Lamb chops, steaks, and burgers were cooked to perfection and served with baked potatoes and homegrown Jersey tomatoes. After work, he poured himself a Dewars on the rocks and smoked an un-filtered Camel cigarette. This was a ritual for him after another day of running the family business—a well-known men's clothing store on Cookman Avenue in Asbury Park. The store was founded by my great-grandfather, Abraham, handed over to my grandfather, Charles, and then passed on to my father, Murray. It would not make it to me.

When dinner was ready, Dad would pour himself a Ballantine Ale to drink at the table. He'd let me taste what was left in his glass of Scotch. I'd take a sip, make a face, and think, *Who in their right mind would drink this stuff?* Apparently I would, as years later I became a Scotch drinker with Dewars as my beverage of choice.

We always had a live-in maid while I was growing up, which was not uncommon in Jewish households at that time. We weren't rich, but I think we pretended to be. My mother never learned how to cook, which was odd considering that her own mother was a fabulous cook. In fact, on the rare occasions that she made dinner, the menu was always scrambled eggs with toast. Afterward, my father would have to scrub the cast iron frying pan with a Brillo pad just to scrape off the remnants of what she had burned. I used to joke that after my mother cooked dinner, we'd have to throw the pan out! She didn't find that very amusing.

In any event, either Isabel or Gladys would prepare amazing meals for us every night. We ate like kings—brisket one night, fried chicken the next, roast beef, and so on. I'm happy to report that my mother did not ring a bell but would just call out, "Gladys, Mr. Levinsohn would like some more." As a treat for my father, we would occasionally have boiled tongue with potatoes and brussels sprouts. He grew up eating Eastern European meals like that. Gladys would carry the serving tray in, and my sister and I would look across the table at each other and roll our eyes. We ate it, but we didn't have to like it!

We always had a salad first with fresh rye bread that my mother would pick up from Freedman's Bakery in Deal. And preceding the salad would usually be half of a pink grapefruit. Gladys would cut the sections for us and place a maraschino cherry in the middle. I liked to sprinkle a little sugar on mine. I told this to my friend Steve Pizza. He grew up in abject poverty in Long Branch and was horrified that somebody else would cut our grapefruit sections for us. If he ever complained about anything in his house, he'd feel the back of his father's hand on his jaw.

The other thing that really got to him was that our parents sent us to sleepaway camp every summer. The camp was located on Spectacle Lake in Kent, Connecticut. There we would play organized sports all day, water ski, sail, and eat really good food. They even had a nine-hole golf course. It was an exclusively Jewish camp with most of the kids coming from Long Island, New York City, and North Jersey. I've often wondered how many captains of industry and Wall Street tycoons emerged from the ranks of that camp's attendees. And as for Steve Pizza, revenge came later in life when the tables were turned, and he became rich and I became poor.

Our obsession with food remains the one constant in our lives. We think about it, we make plans around it, and sometimes even dream about it.

We take food for granted even though millions of human beings are starving all over the world. As is often the case, we don't fully grasp the catastrophic conditions crushing people in faraway lands every day.

Still heading south on the Pacific Coast Highway, I pulled off at San Juan Capistrano to stop at a Rubio's Fish Tacos. Broiled cod on a fresh flour tortilla with warm black beans, cool cabbage, and a choice of toppings from the salsa bar. I added jalapeños, pico de gallo, and a squeeze of lime. With a freshly squeezed lemonade in hand, I sat down at one of the outdoor picnic tables and savored this simple delicacy as a cool Pacific breeze blew over me.

I had been in touch with some friends who'd moved from New Jersey to San Marcos, about twenty miles north of San Diego. Jack O'Brien and I had fought many battles together on the construction sites of Jersey. He had once worked for me as a foreman at DuroCraft Construction, and I became friends with him and his wife, Judy. Upon hearing I would be in the area, they had invited me to stay with them and their kids until I got settled. I could work with Jack in his contracting business whenever he needed help. I was still a good carpenter, and all my tools were packed in my Explorer. Once you've learned a trade, you always possess a valuable asset in your back pocket.

It seemed strange that my trip, which had begun in New Jersey and then crossed the whole country through Memphis, Phoenix, Las Vegas, and Laguna Beach, was ending up in San Diego. Extrapolating that out even further, I contemplated how my whole life had led up to this moment, including my exploits on the Jersey Shore, Kentucky, and Israel. Once again, I was attempting to decipher a chain of events too complex to fully comprehend.

The O'Briens were very gracious to invite me into their home. I didn't know another soul living out there, but a little detail like that had never stopped me before. I had gained a lot of practice at taking things one step at a time. Of course, I had been much younger when I'd last packed up and moved to parts unknown. The real question now was, at forty-two years old, could I settle down and make a life in San Diego?

It turned out that Jack didn't really have much work. We were still in a recession, and even though San Diego was the sixth largest city in the country, things were tight. He'd hustle around and find small renovation work to survive on, and some days he needed me, most days he did not. I looked through the want ads in the *San Diego Union Times* and there might be two or three construction-related jobs. Thankfully, and despite things not working out as planned, I still had enough money left to buy myself some time.

I broke out my olive-green suit and went on a job interview at a stock brokerage firm in downtown San Diego. Raymond James and Associates was one of those boiler room outfits that grind new associates into mincemeat before spitting them out. Some low-level manager was reviewing my resume while I was observing the atmosphere on the trading floor. It looked like Hell Week at the Marine boot camp on Parris Island. Desperate-looking guys were squeezed into cubicles with just a phone and a computer monitor. Bosses were screaming at recruits to cold-call prospective clients using a script seemingly fashioned by black ops psychologists. The newbies even had to ask permission to go to the bathroom. In addition, they started at five in the morning in order to synchronize with the New York markets. This particular interview did not progress too far. It was clear to me that I'd fit in better making tacos with guys who didn't speak English than I would as an intern for these assholes!

As a result of the lack of work, my days consisted of waking up at the O'Briens' to an empty house and going out to breakfast for *huevos rancheros*. Then I drove down the coast, exploring new places along the way. Actually, it was not the worst use of my time.

One day I landed on Coronado Island just south of San Diego. Taking the scenic bridge from the mainland, I found my way to the world-famous Hotel del Coronado. After you wander around a place like this for an afternoon, you feel like you've gone back in time. This landmark hotel had opened in 1888 and is still the second-largest wooden structure in the United States. I tried to imagine what it must've been like to work as a carpenter on a job like that a hundred years ago.

From the start, that project was beset with difficulties—a lack of local materials, a shortage of workers, and an overly complex set of building plans. Chinese immigrants were shipped in from San Francisco to provide cheap labor. Building supplies were floated down on barges from the Pacific Northwest. Additional money was required from investors. When the job was finally completed, it was considered an architectural masterpiece. Like the Hearst Castle, The Del, as it was known, became a premier destination for presidents, business tycoons, and movie stars in the 1920s and '30s. With its temperate climate and pristine beaches, it remains to this day one of the most desirable vacation spots in the country.

These little excursions were enjoyable, but I realized I couldn't continue like this forever. Staying at the O'Briens' was comfortable, but as Ben Franklin famously said, "Guests, like fish, begin to smell after three days." I had already been there a lot longer than that, but so far so good. I got along very well with Judy and her two boys, Matt and Devin. I think Jack felt bad that he didn't have any work for me, but he was fighting for his own survival. I periodically bought groceries and beer, attempting to make at least some contribution to the household.

Then I stumbled upon the Oceanside Card Casino ten miles north of San Marcos. California has long been known for its legalized gambling, with its main focus on the vibrant horse-racing industry. Small, licensed poker rooms were also prevalent throughout the state. What have always been missing were Las Vegas-style casinos. Only Indian reservations were allowed to operate those types of venues.

The Oceanside poker room was like many of the other local establishments—small, comfortable, and mostly populated by the same people day after day. With low overhead, these spots were quite profitable for their owners. I wandered in and looked around. It was the middle of the day on a weekday, and the place was relatively busy. The people at the tables all seemed to know each other. There was a small bar and restaurant attached to it. Waitresses brought players food and beverages and placed them on little tables behind their seats. Everybody seemed to be enjoying themselves.

I started going there a lot. I was a solid and experienced player and immediately felt comfortable seated at the green felt with a stack of chips in front of me. Before long, I was on a first-name basis with the managers, dealers, and waitresses. Employing my Lyle Stuart method of quitting while I was ahead, I was steadily winning modest amounts of money.

The place got very busy at night and on the weekends. They had tournaments, giveaways, and promotional events. I came to realize that this place was the primary social life for many residents in the Oceanside area. Husbands and wives came to play, and all their friends too. For the folks who had the time and money, going to the beach and then afterward to the card casino was a nice way of life. Throw in some good Mexican food, and it was almost heaven! It was certainly a lot mellower than the cold-hearted reptilian vibes of Las Vegas. I could envision my own future living in an existence like this. Of course, a lot of things would have to break my way for that to happen.

CHAPTER TEN

REPENTANCE

T HE JEWISH HIGH HOLY DAYS came late that fall. My father may have been president of our temple, but we weren't particularly religious. We just observed the basic tenets of the religion, as opposed to Orthodox Jews who precisely followed every law written in the Scriptures. I always found it ironic when such deeply religious people were periodically accused in the newspaper of such corrupt practices as welfare and bank fraud.

At thirteen, I celebrated my Bar Mitzvah service at our temple, followed by a big reception in a tent in our backyard. My father hired the Ruby Melnick Trio to provide musical entertainment. This was a huge event, representing the culmination of my Hebrew studies. At age thirteen, in the eyes of my religion, I was now considered a man. Of course, in the eyes of the world, I was just a teenager who couldn't make a move without his parents' permission.

We did not keep a kosher household or pray before we ate or anything like that. We did, however, attend High Holiday services with the visage of great solemnity as we entered the temple hall. It started with Rosh Hashanah, which marks the Jewish New Year. Ten days later, we fasted during Yom Kippur, the holiest day of the year. At least my father and I did—not so sure about my mother and sister. You can't eat anything from sundown to sundown as you seek forgiveness for last year's sins. It is referred to as the Day of Atonement. It's a very serious business, although many of the kids snuck out of services and walked to Richie's Sub Shop on Main Street in Asbury Park. There we would recklessly break our covenant by feasting on Italian hero sandwiches.

As I got older, I became more conscientious about fasting. When I was no longer living at home, I rarely attended services but treated the Day of Atonement with respect. Not eating for twenty-four hours was the least I could do to make up for my countless sins. When I lived in Kentucky and was the only Jew around, I still fasted. When I lived on the kibbutz in Israel, practically everybody was Jewish, but only outsiders like Americans and Europeans fasted. The Israelis living there were secular and observed only the historical aspects of holidays. They actually held the religious fanatics of Israeli society in contempt. Some of those more extreme groups lived in insulated neighborhoods in Jerusalem. If you entered these Orthodox enclaves, it was like stepping back into another century. To hardworking kibbutzniks, these religious zealots were a rung below Arab terrorists.

So now I found myself in San Marcos, living with an Irish Catholic family as sundown for the start of Yom Kippur was fast approaching. I had to eat my dinner before sunset, so I hopped in my car, drove to a local diner, and ate a bowl of pasta. Then I decided to find a temple and listen to the *Kol Nidre* service. This is a beautiful and solemn service for seeking forgiveness. Lord knows I needed it. Yom Kippur was my one chance to wipe the slate clean!

I found a synagogue in a neighboring town in the Yellow Pages and made my way there. I was stopped at the entrance by an old Jewish guy wearing a yarmulke and the traditional tallis draped over his shoulders. He had deep bags under his melancholy eyes and a receding hairline.

He asked me, "Are you a member of Temple Beth Israel?"

I stared into those tired eyes, surprised by his question. I never lied and certainly wasn't going to start now. "No, I'm visiting from New Jersey.

I'm Charles Levinsohn. What's your name?" I was trying the old charm offensive.

"I'm Irving Cohen. Well, Charles, do you have a ticket?"

"A ticket?"

"Yes, you needed to purchase a ticket to attend Kol Nidre, but we're sold out."

"No, I don't have a ticket. As I mentioned before, I'm visiting from out of state. I'm just a Jew who would like to attend services on the High Holidays."

"Well, I'm sorry, but unless you have a ticket or a letter stating that you're a member of a temple in your hometown, I can't let you in."

Never a break! This was like the theater of the absurd. You have to pay to pray? I was no longer a member of a temple, and even if I were, how would I get a letter now? All I wanted to do was sit in the back and seek forgiveness, but this guy wouldn't let me.

I walked away defeated by Irving the Jew. I got back in my car, rolled down the windows, and started driving up the PCH. It was too early to go back to the O'Briens', so I figured I'd just drive and breathe while I fought off the emotion of not belonging anywhere. I couldn't get past thinking, *Is this my destiny, to wander in my own personal Diaspora?*

I passed by Carlsbad, Oceanside, and San Clemente. The air felt good against my skin as I tried to put my existential loneliness behind me. This is a practice that I have become very adept at. After a while, I turned around and headed back toward San Marcos.

The next day, I thankfully woke up to an empty house. No *huevos rancheros* today. I had a lot of time to kill until about 8:00 p.m., when I could eat again. I showered, got dressed, and started driving north. It was a foggy day. I got all the way past Laguna and Newport to Huntington Beach and parked the Explorer to walk through the fog on the endless beach and reflect on everything I'd done in the past year. I tracked it chronologically, starting from last year's Yom Kippur. It was a year of turmoil—my business grinding to a halt during the recession, my attempt to replace lost income through gambling, transient relationships with women. Everything just seemed up in the air. My only saving grace was an inherent sense of calm. Fortunately, I do not possess a hyperactive or overly emotional personality. That's not to say that I never react or even overreact to adversity. It's just that I always find my way back to a peaceful inner center. I'm lucky in that regard.

This trip out West was by far my most significant undertaking of the past year, even though it hadn't really worked out as I had hoped. I had been unable to put down any roots in Arizona, Nevada, or California, but at least I'd had the courage and freedom to have tried.

I walked on that beach for a long time before working my way back down the Pacific Coast Highway. My car almost drove itself to the parking lot of the temple that had shunned my presence the night before. I walked in as if I were invisible. It was the start of the early evening service marking the end of the High Holidays. The period between Rosh Hashanah and Yom Kippur is called the Days of Awe, and I've always liked the poetry of that.

The temple was not nearly as crowded as it had been for the Kol Nidre service. I found a seat on the side, way off in the back. Glancing around, I spotted Irving Cohen on the other side. Either he didn't see me or he had relinquished his role as gatekeeper—or maybe he did see me and just had mercy on the Jew from Jersey. I followed along as the rabbi read out of the prayer book. Then I stood up as directed and listened to the plaintive singing of the choir. Seeing all these Jewish faces flashed me back to my first days on the kibbutz in Israel when I'd studied the Semitic faces of the people there. I was onto something profound, but I couldn't pursue that train of thought just then. I didn't want to think, just wanted to let myself go. We stood and prayed for forgiveness for all our sins from the previous year. I closed my eyes tightly and swayed as I listened to the rabbi's words.

When it was finished, I shook hands with the man sitting next to me and then slowly exited the temple. As I approached the door, I saw Irving Cohen standing there. He nodded at me, and we shook hands without saying a word. My repentance was now complete.

CHAPTER ELEVEN
DEFEATED BUT NOT DESTROYED

THE NEXT DAY, I INFORMED Jack and Judy that I would be leaving soon to return to New Jersey and thanked them for their hospitality. Jack suggested that he and I go out for drinks that night, so we drove into downtown San Diego, to a popular outdoor bar and grill called Acapulco. There was a line to get past some young guy guarding the entrance and checking people's IDs. He had the same job as Irving Cohen! I reached the front of the line, and he asked for my driver's license. I was forty-two years old.

I said, "Really?"

He replied, "My boss said I have to check everybody."

I handed him my ID.

He then announced to the world, "Wow, dude, you're older than my dad!"

Great, I needed that.

Jack's next-door neighbors were a Mexican-American family. The head of the household was Alberto Garcia, and he worked as a masonry contractor. His wife, Rosa, was always bringing homemade Mexican dishes over to Jack and Judy's. They had three nice kids. The weekend before I left, Alberto invited us to take a ride down to Puerta Nueva, which is south of Tijuana in Baja California province. We piled into his truck with its extended cab—all the O'Briens, all the Garcias, and me. We slipped below the San Diego/San Ysidro border crossing and through the heart of Tijuana, onto the coastal road just beyond the town of Rosarita. I had never been to Mexico before. Alberto was taking great pleasure in being our tour guide as he took us to Lobster Village. There we sat, overlooking the big blue Pacific Ocean and drinking beer and eating the world-famous Langosta lobsters, while the kids played Frisbee in a nearby field. It was a fantastic day.

My final trip to the Oceanside Card Casino miraculously ended with my winning a $2,500 poker jackpot, which resuscitated my fading bankroll for the trip home. I bought Jack and Judy a gift certificate for a new Italian restaurant in the upscale neighborhood of La Jolla. The Mexican food in San Diego was out of this world, but the Italian cuisine could not hold a candle to the East Coast.

This new authentic Italian bistro intended to correct that. Ironically, it was called Manhattan.

A few days later, I packed up my Explorer and hit the road again. In no rush, I decided to take the southern route back east. I hugged the Mexican border to Yuma, Arizona, and then on to Interstate 10. The first night, I stayed in a motel in El Paso, Texas. When I started this journey, I had been feeling very hopeful. Now I was returning home defeated but not destroyed. I had not achieved my goal of settling out West. I'd left home around Labor Day, and it was not even Christmas yet. I had only lasted in Vegas until Columbus Day. That fucking idiot savant, Steve Pizza, had predicted it right on the money!

I veered left onto Interstate 20, driving northwest on a diagonal across the entire state of Texas. It's over 800 miles from El Paso to Texarkana and takes almost twelve hours driving time. I don't think I'll ever be doing that again. Two days later, I arrived back on the Jersey Shore. It felt weird at first, almost like a dream. Despite its familiarity, I had briefly been a resident of the West Coast, and now suddenly I was not.

My Ford Explorer had held up surprisingly well despite the wear and tear of such an arduous trip. All things being considered, I'd held up pretty well too. It had been an inspired idea even if it didn't work out as planned. Traveling around from place to place, you realize how big this country is. When you cross the state line from Tennessee into Arkansas, the terrain might change and the accents might sound a little different, but you're still in America. If you cross a similar line of demarcation in Europe, you'd be in another country with an entirely different language and culture. In retrospect, I had visited many cool places and met some interesting people at every leg of the journey. I was sure something positive would come out of this experience, although I had no idea what that might be.

I tell people that if they can find the time, they should take a trip like this at least once in their lifetime. At a minimum, you could fly into San Francisco, rent a car, and drive all the way down the California coast to San Diego. It's an unforgettable experience whether you go alone like I did or with others. I wish I could do it again, but I might be running out of time.

Meanwhile, I put all of that behind me and looked the immediate future squarely in the eye. Starting over on the Jersey Shore wasn't as difficult as it might've been. Suddenly there was a lot of construction work owing to a major tropical storm that had torn through the area while I was gone. I hadn't officially dissolved DuroCraft, and some of the guys were happy to come back to work for me. I found an apartment one block from the beach and sort of fell right back into the same life I'd tried to escape. It wasn't that it was a bad life—far from it. I'd just wanted to take a shot at something new. But I'd failed, and I could live with that.

Round Two of DuroCraft Construction was different from the earlier version. I managed to land bigger jobs with a greater risk/reward quotient. What was not different was the struggle to keep my head above water. This seems to be a recurring theme for me, yet somehow I always seem to survive. That doesn't make me special. Struggle is the nature of our existence. There are haves and have nots, but everybody has problems, rich and poor alike. They're just different problems.

I once again found myself in the familiar territory of being caught in a vise grip between two opposing forces. The guys working for me wanted to be paid more for doing less, while the people I was working for wanted to pay me less for doing more! This was an unsustainable business model. Variations of this exist in many enterprises, but it's exacerbated even more so in the labor market.

My crew and I completed many jobs back then, but it all feels like a dream to me now. Those structures are still standing to prove it, but nobody would remember who built them. They were not exactly Hearst Castle or the Hotel Del Coronado. We were just some guys who arrived in the morning and left in the evening. We battled through the adversity of greedy developers, asshole building inspectors, and our own human error. That last one ultimately fell on my shoulders. Heavy is the crown when you're in charge of a bunch of misfits doing manual labor. These jobs were more complex than I was accustomed to, so I was forced to learn new techniques on the fly. I found myself in a minefield where opportunities for error were like rattlesnakes waiting in the tall grass. You never saw them coming.

Occasionally after work, I'd stop for a drink at one of the many go-go bars located on my way home. After getting paid on Fridays, our whole crew would go for cocktails to Heartbreakers in Asbury Park. The bar would be packed, music would be playing, and sexy girls would be dancing on the stage. Money, alcohol, and pretty women were the reward for surviving another week of back-breaking work. I used to run into other contractors I knew who were recovering from another painful day on the job. We bought each other drinks as the conversations invariably drifted to the topic of getting ripped off by the people holding the purse strings. Some guys had some truly nightmarish experiences that scarred them for years. I was ripped off from time to time, but never as bad as some of those guys. I eventually came out broke but with my spirit still intact.

I met a guy who built railroad tie walls on hilly properties, usually for big developers. This required engineering experience and heavy machinery. These walls prevented mudslides and other disastrous occurrences, and he was really good at it. The problem though, was his personality. Jeff was a pushy Brooklyn Jew who alienated people without even trying. We had met on a big condo project where I was working as a job super, and we quickly became friends. He invited me to his house to have dinner with his family and grilled lamb chops in the backyard while we drank beer. Outside of the combative arena of the construction site, he was a good-hearted guy. He took me to his weekly poker game, where I soon became a regular. He had purchased tickets for a Bob Dylan concert at Madison Square Garden and asked if I wanted to go. Since Dylan was one of my heroes, I gladly accepted.

The developers of the project hated Jeff because of his abrasive manner. They often held up his money just to aggravate him. I advised him to just shut up and play the game, reminding him that the only reason he was doing this was to support his family and pay his crew.

On top of it, he had made some real estate investments that didn't quite pan out. He became overextended and lost his ability to buy more railroad ties at the local lumberyard. His outstanding balance exceeded his credit limit. So, he asked me if he could buy some railroad ties and charge it to my account, which was in good standing. As a friend, I agreed, but I wanted to know the limit of what he would charge. "No more than $5,000, and I'll pay you back when the job is finished," he promised. This is how friendships end. He charged almost $20,000 to my account and was unable to pay me back. Being an optimist, he felt that if he could just buy some time, then things would turn around. This point of view is not uncommon among self-made men. Unfortunately for me, his failed strategy placed me in a bad fucking spot.

I got sent for to meet with the finance manager of the lumberyard. It was like being called into the principal's office in high school, although in this case, the manager was a super nice guy. Part of his job was to help guys who had fallen behind in their payments, which was a common dilemma for small building contractors. So here I was, sitting across from Al, the finance manager, trying to resolve this issue created by my friend. Al is probably dead now given that this was thirty years ago, and he was an old guy back then. I don't say this to be morbid. It just makes me realize how every crisis passes, and then a new crisis replaces it. In a sense, it's all an illusion, yet I didn't think sharing that philosophy with Al was going to improve my situation.

Al proposed a solution for me to work off the debt by building extensive shelving and flooring in several large barns that housed the lumber. He and his boss made the terms so favorable that I'd be able to pay my guys their weekly salaries while simultaneously reducing my balance. They could've been hard asses and threatened collections, but they took a human approach instead. I will never forget it. As a postmortem, I also never got a dime from Jeff. We lost touch, and I don't know what became of him. He's probably still out there battling the galactic forces aligned against him.

I then caught a break when Big Tony asked me to work on a restaurant renovation owned by a mutual friend. Basil Plasteras was a well-known personality on the Jersey Shore. He came from a very prominent Greek family and owned a popular restaurant, the Squire's Pub. He was very fond of my family. My grandfather had been his father's attorney. More importantly, his late brother George had dated my sister in high school. George was an All-American hero—football star, scholar, and all-around great guy. He went to Brown University on a football scholarship, but he developed leukemia and tragically died. Basil had a big heart, and the memory of his dearly departed brother occupied a lot of space there.

This job would be what we called T&M—time and material. I would supply a carpentry crew, and Basil would pay me an hourly rate for each guy. Big Tony would supply the material. I was able to tack on overhead and profit on each of my guys. As long as they provided stellar craftsmanship in a timely manner, everything would be fine. In other words, I couldn't lose money.

Basil was a big man, upward of 300 pounds. He would stand on the edge of the construction area with his arms folded, watching the job progress. He always wore a dress shirt under his brightly colored V-neck sweater, size triple XL. Physically, he reminded me of the Turkish prison warden in *Midnight Express*, the difference being that Basil was a teddy bear, and that guy was a fucking sadist. In fact, Basil instructed his chef to prepare lunch every day for all the plumbers, painters, and carpenters. Charcoal-broiled cheeseburgers one day, strip steaks the next, fried chicken the next. It was an unbelievable gesture. That's just how he was. I wanted to make sure my crew did the right thing, so if I saw somebody standing around, I would tell him to look busy even if he was legitimately waiting for someone to bring him material. On this job, appearances mattered.

In the end, Basil and Big Tony were very happy with the finished product. The night before the grand reopening, Basil invited everybody who had worked there to a celebratory dinner. His chef prepared steak and lobster tails for everybody. This kind of generosity is virtually unheard of in this normally cutthroat business. Basil is no longer with us, but he will never be forgotten.

CHAPTER TWELVE

THE LAST HURRAH

T HE FINAL EPISODE OF DuroCraft Construction came right on the heels of the Squire's Pub job. Big Tony asked me to bid on the carpentry labor for a new municipal building in South Jersey. He warned me to keep my estimate at the bare minimum because he had to be the low bidder in order to get the job. That should've set off a red flag right there. Big Tony had an interesting philosophy. He believed guys should work for him for less because he always paid on time. His competitors were a slew of Greek general contractors who never paid on time. In other words, he wanted a discount just for doing the right thing! I found this to be almost insane. If we did the work, we were supposed to get paid. You're not doing me a special favor by meeting your moral and business obligation. In the deep recesses of his mind, he had convinced himself that this was a fair deal. I knew that he needed me because we always showed up and did a good job, but he also knew that I needed the work. In this poker game, he held the upper hand. He had a lot of chips, and I did not. Once again, "Money talks and bullshit walks."

I bid the job too low. I knew it for a fact when he rushed to have the contract drawn up. He practically ran to the copy machine. And if you ever saw him run, it wasn't a pretty sight. He was one of my closest friends, but he couldn't sign that contract fast enough! Being an optimist, I thought I'd just use a smaller crew with a lighter payroll and work as efficiently as possible. That turned out to be a pipe dream. Big Tony installed his partner's younger, inexperienced brother as the job superintendent. This was a problem. Curt was a nice guy, but he screwed up repeatedly, costing me thousands of dollars. He never finished anything he started, which impeded my goal of job efficiency. It ended up with my carpenters either stopping and starting a task or just standing around waiting altogether. Because it was a state job, I was forced to pay union wages, which were twice as high as private work. It was good for my crew but bad for me, especially if we couldn't keep moving. Even though my guys were getting paid for doing nothing due to Curt's incompetence, they didn't want to see me get fucked over. I was a good boss who had treated them well, and if I went down, they went down too. And this job was turning into the *Titanic*.

I've often said that the construction business is a business of mistakes. The challenge is how fast you recognize them and how quickly you correct them. I was the head of a crew that varied in size from four carpenters to as many as a dozen. There were often multiple ways of approaching a particular problem. As the boss, I didn't always have to be right, just as long as *somebody* was right. I usually worked my way to the correct solution unless some aberration jumped up and bit me on the ass.

As it turned out, this whole job turned into one big fucking aberration! It started with the problems created by Curt's inexperience but then shifted unexpectedly into what could only be described as the twilight zone. Every day I drove an hour from home, arriving at the job at 7:45 for an 8:00 a.m. start. My guys were always on time too. One morning as I turned down the street leading to the site, there was a mob of guys on both sides of the road screaming at us. They were union carpenters demonstrating in protest that we had taken their jobs. They even had this thirty-foot-high blow-up rat representing our betrayal of the working man. This charming invention was taken from place to place wherever union guys had a grievance. The only problem for them was that our working on this state job was perfectly legal. It's called prevailing wage work and is based on the Davis-Bacon Act of 1931, and it allows nonunion employees to work on state funded jobs if they are paid wages commensurate to the union scale. In fact, I had to pay my guys even more because they also received the value of union benefits on top of their base wages. My guys loved prevailing wage jobs. Instead of making twenty dollars an hour on our private jobs, now they were making forty. These jobs could also be profitable for me if nothing major went wrong. But something always went wrong—it just depended how bad it was.

So now, every morning we had to drive through a gauntlet of screaming maniacs and a blow-up rat. They thought we were scabs, but we weren't. Scabs are guys who go to work on jobs where union guys are striking for higher wages. That was not the case here. Their corrupt leaders were just unhappy because they weren't getting a cut of the action. They believed that only union guys had the right to work. It's an age-old debate in the labor market that has periodically spawned violence in the streets, most notably from groups like the Teamsters Union under the late Jimmy Hoffa.

So, we had a weak job superintendent, Union protestors, delayed deliveries of materials—add it all up, and I was under a *lot* of pressure. I was paying out a lot of money every day and not getting enough work done to justify it. It wasn't the fault of my crew, who were doing everything in their power to move things along. In all honesty, I also made some critical mistakes in my estimating and analysis of the job. Big Tony may have planted the seed of low-balling the cost of labor, but I missed a couple of key details in the complex architectural plans. I was not formally trained in this area, but that was no excuse for my oversights. I had enough experience under my belt to get it right, but I did not. There was one item that was very labor-intensive that I assumed was the responsibility of the Portuguese masonry subcontractor. I was incorrect, so I had to eat it. As a side note, I had worked with these Portuguese bricklayers on many other occasions. Nicest guys in the world. We helped each other out whenever we could—but in this case, it was all on me.

Then an Act of God entered the equation. It was on a Friday about a month into the job. We had just raised the roof and braced all the rafters before we went home for the weekend. When we returned on Monday, the whole roof was lying in a pile on the ground. A tropical storm had blown through the area over the weekend with fifty-mile-per-hour winds ripping the roof right off the building. As we unknowingly pulled up on Monday morning, the union guys were deliriously cheering at our misfortune in a sick display of human cruelty.

"Character is destiny." That famous quote was invoked by the Greek philosopher, Heraclitus, 2,500 years ago. It seemed kind of relevant to me then. I was being put to the test for reasons unknown. That saying would be seared into my brain for future reference.

We salvaged the smashed-up roof trusses and reconstructed the building. Meanwhile, those scumbag union activists used their local muscle to have a safety inspector walk around the job harassing me. In addition, a local biased newspaper came and interviewed me. It ended up being a hit piece in which they maliciously published my name, home address, and photos of the job. Fuck them!

Big Tony's partner on the job was Russ, who was Curt's older brother. The final blow was when Russ refused to pay me for repairing the roof from the storm. I was running out of money and had passed the point of no return. I almost came to blows with Russ, and for the first time in my life, I walked off the job. Big Tony was in a precarious spot. He was my friend and knew I was getting screwed, but his bread was buttered at his partner's table. He did not intervene on my behalf.

I was now officially disgusted with this business and made the decision to terminate DuroCraft Construction. I was forty-five years old and tired of the endless struggles in a game that seemed like it would never be tilted in my favor. Many guys have had great success in the contracting business, and many others have washed out. I had chosen a specific niche of providing carpentry labor to big contractors. This conscious decision placed me in a debilitating vise grip from two different directions. It's only human to feel like a victim when the deck is stacked against you. That emotion cannot be indulged for very long though—it just leads to bitterness, which benefits no one.

Ultimately, I am accountable for my own actions, hence my reference to the quote by Heraclitus. I was fortunate that I had built up enough character in the tobacco fields of Kentucky and the fishponds of Israel to withstand a setback on a construction site in Jersey. All my experiences up to this point had hardened me into a vessel of perseverance.

Several months later, I was paid a visit by a representative from the New Jersey Department of Labor. Three guys whom I'd hired specifically to install all the plywood on the building had registered a complaint. They claimed that I hadn't paid them the prevailing wage. I thought I had a leg to stand on since I'd hired them for a fixed price as independent subcontractors. Two of the guys I had met on a previous job for Big Tony. I liked them personally and thought highly of their work ethic, but their ringleader was a scumbag. I'd seen it in his eyes, but he was an experienced carpenter, so

I'd let it go. He led the coup against me and filed the complaint.

My interview with the Department of Labor guy was very amiable, especially when he discovered that I had known his late father. I provided all the documentation he requested and answered all his questions. We parted with a hearty handshake, and he assured me that everything looked in order.

About two weeks later, I received a registered letter from the Department of Labor demanding that I immediately pay $26,000 to be dispersed among the three traitors. I looked long and hard at that letter. First of all, I didn't have $26,000, and second, there was no way I would ever agree to this. I went bust on that fucked-up job while Big Tony's company probably made hundreds of thousands of dollars. I called him up and said that I would get in my car and drive out West rather than pay a single dime. In the end, it was Big Tony's job, and all responsibility ultimately landed on him. He went to the Labor office and negotiated a deal with them. He paid $13,000 to settle the matter.

After the debacle of that last job, it was a miracle that Big Tony and I remained friends. I was still invited to his family functions, and we still played in the same weekly poker game together. When his wife tragically died, I attended her funeral. As his many older siblings slowly passed away, I went to every wake. My old friend Rich commented, "Wow, he put you out of business, and you still think he's a great guy. He must be really good!" John, who runs the weekly poker game, more sarcastically remarked, "A lot of guys who worked for Big Tony are selling insurance now." That last statement would turn out to be prophetic.

I decided there was no future in doing back-breaking work any longer and sold off most of my tools and equipment. Some guys can work construction into their late sixties, but I was not going to be one of them. Carrying the heavy end of a forty-foot girder through frozen mud was not what I envisioned for my future. It was time once again to try something new, but I had no idea what that would be. I was proud of what I had accomplished at DuroCraft and the relationships I had forged. I'd built a reputation for excellence and honesty, while providing jobs to a revolving door of both misfits and master carpenters. I may have suffered from the financial hardships of the construction business, but I had ripped off no one. I often said, "The money comes and goes but only the work remains." All those decks I'd constructed in my early days enhanced the lifestyle of many homeowners. And the bigger projects I'd worked on are still standing as a quiet testament to the fact that I was here and that I built something.

CHAPTER THIRTEEN

S O NOW IT WAS TIME to transition from arm power to brain power. No more wearing muddy work boots and torn jeans with a heavy tool belt around my waist. Instead of chasing money in vain as I had for all those years, I'd plant myself right in the middle of it.

I broke out my trusty green suit and paisley tie and arranged some job interviews. It wasn't like this was my lucky outfit or anything. I had failed miserably while wearing it on those fucked-up interviews out West. But it was my only suit, and now I was on my home court. I'd just turn on the old Kentucky charm, which admittedly hadn't worked out that great so far. If it had, I wouldn't have found myself once again at the mercy of some office recruiter.

My first meeting was at a local stock brokerage firm, Dean Witter. This experience was not as disheartening as the one at Raymond James and Associates in San Diego, where sadistic managers abused subpar interns with punishments not unlike the practice of Code Red in *A Few Good Men.*

I made a good first impression, so they had me take some aptitude tests and fill out a lot of paperwork. I sat there for what seemed like an eternity, struggling through this assignment. My tie was starting to choke me as beads of sweat formed on my forehead. I wanted to run for the hills! I found the office atmosphere with all these cubicles and computers completely stifling. It was diametrically opposed to the healthy outdoor life I had led for over twenty years. I left the forms on the manager's desk and walked out the door, never to return.

I needed to regroup from that torture chamber, so I went for a walk on the beach. As I meandered along barefoot in the sand, I could breathe again. I slowly dragged my feet through the edge of the surf as I'd done a thousand times before. My thoughts drifted to the topic of money, which not surprisingly was the cause of my current discontent. My normally useless degree in philosophy kicked in as I examined my personal relationship with the undisputed driving force of the universe, the accumulation of wealth. Or in my case, just basically scrounging together enough dough to pay my bills.

As previously chronicled, I did not choose the traditional path laid out for an intelligent young man from an upper middle-class Jewish family. I just had to go cut tobacco in the sweltering fields of Kentucky. Then it was on to dragging heavy nets of fish through muddy ponds on the Mediterranean coast of Israel. My evolution would not be complete until I was dropped headfirst into the quicksand of the Jersey Shore construction industry.

Looking back, it would've been so easy to just go to law school like my parents wanted. Stability, respect, affluence—who in their right mind wouldn't want that? Apparently not me! I thought I knew better, but as it turned out, I knew nothing. And now I found myself at a crossroads as some middle-aged guy whose heavy lifting days were behind him. I needed money to survive and to face an uncertain future that was bearing down on me like a freight train. It wasn't too late—I just needed an attitude adjustment to fit into a world that I'd escaped from with all the urgency of a prison break.

I drove to Monmouth Mall and bought a new suit, then put the green one into mothballs like they do with old battleships that have outlived their usefulness. Like my velour shirt from The Voltaires, it became a collector's item. I was making a fresh start and willing to do whatever was necessary. And what was necessary landed me at an insurance agency owned by our former next-door neighbor, Harry.

Harry had founded the business, and his two sons now ran it. Richie and Alan were each a couple of years younger than me, but they remembered that I was smart in high school, and that seemed to carry a lot of weight with them. It also didn't hurt that I was friendly with one of their biggest producers, whose glowing endorsement sealed the deal. They offered me the job, and I accepted. I was now an insurance salesman! *God help me.*

My old friend Rich lent me some money to embark on my new career. I traded in my work van from DuroCraft and bought a used Cadillac Eldorado. "Fake it 'til you make it" was my new motto. Central casting was calling, so I headed back to the mall for more suits and ties and belts and shoes. I had brown shoes to go with brown slacks and black shoes to go with gray ones. I kept them shined like mirrors. As for shirts, I was forced to buy custom-made because my neck was too big for the ones on the shelves. I guess those decades of grunt work had turned me into half man, half bull. They added little monograms with my initials on the sleeves. It was a nice touch.

Then I got a twenty-dollar haircut and a supply of Gillette razor blades to keep my face smooth and clean-shaven every day. You have to smell good too, so I checked out the samples of cologne at the fragrance counter. I didn't want anything too strong. I'd been around guys who overdid it with that stuff, and it was repulsive, somehow having the reverse effect of what they were going for. I settled on Paco Rabanne, which was pleasant but not overwhelming. It might even arouse some of the attractive females who worked at the agency! I might've been getting a little ahead of myself with that.

First day on the job, I burst through the doors like a movie star announcing to the world that I had arrived. Upon inquiring with the front desk about where I should go, the receptionist said, "Follow me. You'll be working over here." She led me to what was referred to as the "bullpen"—a series of small cubicles outfitted with only a desk and a phone. I quickly learned that my initial mission was to call everybody I knew and try to make appointments without revealing what it was about. Then I would bring an experienced agent with me and keep my mouth shut as he broke the news to the poor bastard that it was about life insurance.

Soon after arriving, I was introduced to my new sales manager, Peter. I was to meet with him daily to establish my goals and advance my training. I knew him a little bit from when we were young. He grew up in Deal, the next town over, and was a member of my mother's beach club, which I visited on occasion. I had recently spotted him there bopping around the pool with his wife and three daughters.

I didn't dislike him, but I didn't like him either. I guess I was neutral until proven otherwise. He was a couple of years younger than me, and now he was my manager. This probably didn't bode well because I quickly established a reputation as being "uncoachable," primarily because I was an independent thinker. After all, I had run a construction company with a crew of maniacs straight out of *The Sopranos*. I could not take directions from guys who never even got their hands dirty. I may not have known anything about the insurance business, but I still thought I was smarter than everybody else. Was this my fatal flaw or my greatest strength? To this day, I honestly still don't know the answer to that.

This was a big firm with about seventy-five people working there, including the salesmen, managers, specialists, and staff. Everybody walked around looking very busy. The guys were all wearing suits, starched shirts, and colorful ties like a lot of thought clearly went into the selection of those outfits every morning. It was ironic that my late father had owned a prominent men's clothing store in Asbury Park, and when I left home for college, my wardrobe had consisted of the conservative brands featured in his store. But it hadn't taken long for me to reject that style and adopt the radical fashions of the hippie culture. He had been horrified. And now here I was, years later, back in the fold. Maybe he'd have been proud of my be-lated return to the traditions he'd once espoused—or maybe not. His pride in my circuitous journey might have required more than me buying a few suits with borrowed money.

I looked around and saw that sitting a few cubes away was a guy I knew from high school. In fact, he was the older brother of Rich, who had lent me the seed money for this new endeavor. Mike was a family man who was working on his third or fourth career. He'd begun there a few months before me and seemed to already know the ropes. A few weeks earlier, I had run into the owners, Richie and Alan, at a diner, and they'd told me Mike had started working for them. They said, and I quote, "We can't wait to get him firing on all cylinders." I looked over at Mike who had his feet up on his desk, holding a manual called *The Beginner's Guide to Selling Life Insurance*. This was mandatory read-ing for all new agents. He had secretly tucked a golf magazine inside it and was studying tips on how to improve his short game. He did not appear to be "firing on all cylinders." He put the magazine down and said, "C'mon, let's go to lunch."

I naïvely asked, "Do we have to be back at a certain time?"

He said, "Don't worry about it. They have no idea what's going on."

And this was the guy who would be guiding my new career.

Lunch was the biggest event of the day at this place. More thought went into this than anything actually related to business. Like two knuckleheads, we brainstormed our countless options, and this routine would be repeated every day.

"Where do you wanna go?" I asked, though sometimes he asked it first.

"I don't know. Where do you wanna go?"

"You feel like Perkins Pancakes, Irv's Deli, or maybe the Chinese buffet?"

"Let's try that new Mexican place in Freehold."

"That's pretty far. Who's gonna drive?"

"I don't care. I'll drive."

Now that we had that pinned down, we could temporarily escape the humiliation of being two middle-aged guys attempting to start new careers with bad attitudes.

For the record, Mike and I were not the only ones in the office who considered lunch to be the highlight of the day. The parking lot would empty out in a mad rush as little cliques of future diners piled into cars streaming toward the exit. Even the owners would head over to their fancy country club to schmooze with other big shots over Dewars on the rocks and steak sandwiches.

Occasionally there would be an agency meeting scheduled during our sacred lunchtime.

Management loved to have meetings on any topic under the sun. These guys actually thought meetings were extremely valuable training tools. Of course, we thought they were a total waste of time. Distrust hovered over the hallways of this office like a black cloud while lukewarm leadership tried to motivate pessimistic people teetering on their second and third careers. The washout rate in this industry was extremely high, hovering around 75 percent. Only newly hired car salesmen had less staying power.

Legend has it that back in the day, Harry had possessed natural leadership qualities. He founded the firm after World War II and hired a small legion of hungry salesmen who would follow him through the Gates of Hell. It was a different era then, marked by heavy drinking, looser regulations, and sales techniques that might be considered unethical by today's standards. Harry and his crew thrived in that environment. Things were good, and they made the most of it. But eventually things changed. The original sales force was getting old. By the time I got there, Harry himself was pushing eighty. The mantle of responsibility was thrust on his sons, who were not natural-born leaders. As much as Richie and Alan tried, they could not inspire the troops. Their well-intentioned but hollow words had the reverse effect, resulting in resentment, sarcasm, and subversive meetings behind closed doors.

I personally had renounced a robust lifestyle of outdoor physical labor to land in this veritable snake pit of cynicism. It was here in this reptilian wilderness that easy money could be made for those who could adapt to conditions on the ground. Cold calling, networking, and aggressive sales practices were necessary tools for success. I had sculpted myself into looking the part of a successful agent with adjustments to my appearance, a new wardrobe, and trading my tool-filled work truck for a nice car. But did I have the temperament? I was once told that I didn't even have the temperament to play golf!

Like any other office, there was a cast of characters who were all fair game to the mockery of jaded cynics like us. Mike and I showed no mercy on these pitiable targets who experienced the venom of our own self-loathing. It was easy to understand why there were so many TV sitcoms based on settings just like this. After all the high-minded things I had experienced in life, this was not among my proudest moments.

As it turned out, my new manager, Peter, and I became good friends. He had some idiosyncrasies that drove me crazy, but he was a good-hearted guy who had become successful in spite of a history of personal adversity. I initially went out on the road with him to observe how he handled sales calls. Later on, we worked on accounts together. More importantly, we always stopped for a big lunch. We often feasted on sushi, and that alone would validate our entire day.

The women on the administrative staff were smarter and usually ate salads in the office lunchroom. The salesmen may have brought in the money, but it was the ladies who made the firm run like clockwork. I went out of my way to always treat them with the respect they deserved. On the other hand, I observed the different salesmen and could tell who was full of shit and who told the truth. Around here, you were only as good as your last sale. I of course had not yet made a sale, but with my flawless understanding of the human condition, I was destined to be a star in this business. I was merely biding my time until fortune smiled on me.

I also learned a valuable tool that saved me from undue criticism from management. When walking around the office, one should always carry a file or a sheet of paper in hand. The importance of this cannot be overstated. It gave you a sense of purpose even if you were just wandering aimlessly and killing time. Appearances were half the battle in a place like this, and I became a master of appearances. I was not particularly proud of that, but I was just trying to avoid conflict until my ship came in. That would happen sooner than I thought.

My big break came unexpectedly at a weekend tennis game. I had been invited to join a group of older guys who played every weekend on the estate of a well-known New York real estate developer. Jack was actually more than well-known—he was characterized in an article in the *New York Times Magazine* as part of Manhattan's real estate royalty. He donated his time and money to many philanthropic causes. The banner waiting at the finish line of the New York Marathon bore the logo of his company. He even donated an elephant to the Bronx Zoo, which he named after his father, Samuel. Jack had known both of my parents for many years and was still fond of my mother, whom he frequently saw at the beach club. After the tennis match, he asked me what I was doing with myself. I told him that I had left the construction business to sell life insurance.

He asked, "What does someone have to do to get a life insurance policy?"

As a man of great wealth, I assumed he had purchased life insurance over the years for personal and estate protection. As the head of a big organization, he probably had someone from his company handle such matters.

I may have been a novice, but I gave him a straight answer. "First you determine how much you need and for how long. Then you fill out an application. After that, the company medically underwrites you via a paramedical exam and your personal physician's report. Based on the information, the underwriters decide whether to approve your application. The whole process generally takes about a month."

Jack asked, "What company do you represent?"

"New England Life."

"That's a reputable company. My first wife passed away several years ago, and I recently remarried. I'd like to purchase a policy to provide for my new wife at the time of my passing. Can you get me some information on a million-dollar policy? I'll give you the name and number of the guy in my office who handles this."

There I was, standing in tennis shorts with a New York real estate tycoon, discussing the possibility of landing my first big sale. With no idea if this would materialize, I was excited. I mean, I'd only been on the job for about a month! Jack could have asked any number of big shot agents in Manhattan to take care of this, and they would have salivated at the chance. I felt honored that a man of his stature would ask me. Now I just had to figure out how to do it! I applied the same principles as in every other undertaking in my life—just put my head down, tell the truth, and push on. Admittedly, I've driven off the road into ditches following those simple instructions, but it's still a good motto.

The next day at work, I told Peter about this fortuitous opportunity. As my manager, it would reflect well on him if one of his new agents succeeded. Word soon spread like wildfire through the office that the new guy was working on a big case, and suddenly I had a lot of new friends. Guys I barely knew expressed concern that an inexperienced agent like me might fuck it up. They graciously offered to partner up with me for half the commission. Their motives were not exactly altruistic, but it didn't make them bad people. They were just trying to make a buck. It didn't matter though, because I was determined to work on this alone. Maybe it would work out or maybe it wouldn't, but I had the confidence in myself to see it through. When you've held your own working side by side with Israeli commandos in waist-deep mud, you're not intimidated by paperwork and phone calls.

It turned out to be a rather complex process owing to the age and health of the applicant. It also required the creation of a special trust for this particular kind of policy. This was obviously unfamiliar territory for me. Then I remembered the first time I had to build a set of stairs. It was complicated, but I concentrated, and one day later, I was walking up those stairs. Step by step everything progressed and finally, after two months, Jack was approved. All that remained was the payment of the annual premium.

Peter was excited because he would receive a nice managerial bonus for my efforts. I was happy for him except that every single day he'd ask, "Did you get the check yet? Did you get the check?"

"No, Peter, they said to call next week."

"Well, why don't you just call today?"

"No, I don't want to be a pest. Now stop bugging me." My instincts were correct, and true to their word, the policy was paid the following week.

I temporarily became kind of a folk hero in the halls of the agency. A brand-new guy had sold the biggest policy of the year and did it without any help from anybody. Naturally, there was some jealousy and sarcasm seeping out of the darker corners of the office. Pettiness is inevitable in a place like this, but fuck 'em! All I knew was that with one sale, I had solidified my immediate future and paid back the money I owed Rich. Of course, now the big question was, what will I do for an encore? It occurred to me that I might just be a one-hit wonder.

I cast my net to a wide array of prospects—people I knew from construction, friends of friends, and total strangers. The afterglow of my big sale lasted for a while, but opening and closing new cases was not easy. You can't make people sign applications just because you need to make your quota. Maybe high-pressure guys could pull that shit off, but not me. Cutting tobacco was hard work. Catching fish in heavy nets was hard work. Running a construction crew full of knuckleheads was hard work. But cold calling strangers to sell them insurance was a nightmare.

In their infinite wisdom, management gave new agents prepared scripts to use on cold calls. The language was unnatural and made you sound like an idiot. Some nitwit from the home office got paid to create a model that predicted how many appointments these scripts would generate. I was forty-five years old and didn't need some bean counter from Boston to tell me how to talk to people. I don't mean to sound like a know it all, but even by then, I already knew one thing—if you can't be yourself, then what's the point? I admit that waltzing around in monogrammed shirts while driving a used Eldorado was not entirely in keeping with "being myself." But those were just accessories, and my essence remained intact. I was the same guy who could play tennis with captains of industry or drink whiskey with the dregs of society. I realized that everyone is just playing the hand they've been dealt. The "haves" and the "have nots" may be holding different cards, but they still have more in common than meets the eye. At some point, everyone realizes their days on Earth are numbered. This is the common ground that forces rich and poor into the same boat on a stormy sea. With waves crashing all around, wins and losses become forgotten entries in dusty ledgers. Nothing lasts, and everything fades away.

I remember visiting Jack's office in New York and seeing the walls filled with photos of him shaking hands with celebrities from all walks of life—politicians, sports figures, titans of industry. Jack has been gone for several years now, and his executive suite may be occupied by the next person in the line of succession. I wonder where those photos are now. Are they still on those hallowed walls or have they been packed away and placed in storage?

These are interesting philosophical questions, but at that point in my life, I had more pressing business at hand. I needed to find someone to sign on the dotted line. My future depended on it!

I actually wasn't a bad salesman. One of the owners said I was "consultative," whatever that meant. I think it was his way of saying that I wasn't pushy enough for his taste. Some other sales agent who had been there for a couple of years invited me to lunch at the Chinese buffet. Over wonton soup and eggrolls, he offered his sage advice, "Just listen to Alan and Richie. They're the owners, and they know what they are talking about. Don't try to reinvent the wheel." He was a nice guy, but behind his back, everyone disrespected him. Shortly thereafter, he was let go for not making his quota. So much for blind loyalty.

I, on the other hand, received a fake wood plaque with a gold-plated inscription hailing me as "1995 New Agent of the Year." What an honor! From a nearly bankrupt builder to Insurance Agent of the Year! But that was already yesterday's news.

The biggest problem for me in a business like this was my slow-moving nature. I have always hated to rush. I don't rush when I wake up, I don't rush to get to work, and by the time I get there, it's almost time for lunch. They were not paying a salary, but the optics still weren't good. I managed to be productive and even won a couple more of those stupid plaques, but there was something about me that just irked the owners. I couldn't really blame them. I set a poor example. I was not disruptive or anything, but they resented independent thinkers who didn't march in lockstep with their infallible vision.

I was forced to overcome my aversion to rushing when I was in the construction business, but that was different. It was my company, and I had responsibilities that superseded personal habits—employees, payrolls, and deadlines. However, in my current situation, I was a commissioned sales agent, essentially a free agent. If I made my quota and didn't act like an asshole, then there really wasn't much to talk about. I routinely achieved those benchmarks but still never transcended my persona as a lifelong underachiever. That character flaw would eventually catch up to me, but not before I hit another home run.

CHAPTER FOURTEEN
A TASTE OF THE GOOD LIFE

M Y UNOFFICIAL MENTOR WAS ROY, who had initially endorsed my hiring. He was about twenty years older than me and one of the remaining agents from Harry's old crew. He was highly successful and had made his bones when the insurance business was still like the Wild West. My father had been friendly with Roy's brother, Mort, who owned a fishing boat and would frequently invite my father out on weekend excursions. My father loved that boat. He even took a course to get his captain's license. Not that he was going to ever buy a boat. He had already fallen on hard times, but he could assume captain's duties if Mort had too much to drink. I went out a few times on those trips. I have vivid memories of getting up early and riding with my father to the marina. He would stop at the deli and buy roast beef sandwiches on rye with mustard and two six packs of Ballantine Ale.

So there I was, sitting in Roy's office, discussing a potential "joint work" opportunity. It was common in this office for a couple of agents to team up on specific sales projects. These efforts often ended in bad blood that lasted for years, but I didn't see that possibility happening with me and Roy.

We were both friendly with a lawyer named Morris, who was a senior partner at one of the most prestigious law firms in the state. I knew him from both the beach club and our Sunday morning tennis games. Mo, as he was called, was an unassuming guy, but he carried a lot of weight at his firm. If Mo was willing to arrange a meeting with us, perhaps Roy and I would see an opening to do some business. It was certainly worth a shot.

Mo liked me. He invited me and my current girlfriend, Laura, to his annual Super Bowl party and even invited us to dinner at Hollywood Country Club, an elite establishment with a first-class golf course, tennis courts, and dining facilities. It catered exclusively to the affluent local Jewish community. There was another country club almost adjacent to Hollywood that was established strictly for wealthy local Christians. This whole lifestyle of golf tournaments and social galas was light years away from my reality.

I put on a blue blazer and slacks and picked up Laura, and we met Mo and his wife Sylvia there. She was a very nice woman. They have both since passed away as many from their generation have. In fact, everyone from that tennis group is gone now, including Roy, who sadly passed away just this year at the age of ninety-three.

Prior to getting seated in the lavish dining room, the members and their guests traditionally retired to the cocktail lounge for drinks and appetizers served by white-jacketed waiters. The four of us sat at a small table, chatting and sipping our cocktails. I ordered a Dewars on the rocks and looked around, observing that the members were in good spirits as the men shook hands and slapped each other on the back. They kissed their friends' wives on the cheek, and the women kissed each other as well. Both the men and the women were dressed immaculately. A lot of thought went into the selection of these outfits, as they clearly wanted to look attractive to their peers. They looked good, and they smelled good as intoxicating fragrances wafted through the room. This was the definition of the good life. I had to admit that I admired the sense of comradery that existed there. This would never be a part of my life, but I did not look upon it with any cynicism or jealousy. I got it. Perhaps if I had turned right instead of left, I might have been clinking glasses there with a partner from my own law firm. I had entertained such fantasies from time to time, but only to a point. There is no payoff in traveling too far down the road of regret. This was a pleasant evening, and I appreciated Mo inviting us into his world, even if only for a moment.

As it turned out, I ended up spending more time at Hollywood. My sales manager, Peter, was the treasurer of the club and would occasionally invite me there for lunch. The food at this place was phenomenal. It was expensive to belong to a club like this, and the members were extremely high maintenance. They demanded only the best and always got what they wanted. And yet they still complained.

Whenever I went there, I observed a table in the back reserved for a group of old timers. They ate lunch at the club everyday—Manhattan clam chowder, shrimp cocktails, steak sandwiches, and so on. They shared war stories from their businesses, admired some of the younger women (who in their case might be well into their 70s), and gossiped about other members. Afterward, they might go to the clubhouse and play gin for a couple of hours. When it was time to leave, the valet parking guys would run like the wind to fetch their cars because older guys were good tippers. Tomorrow would be another day in Paradise. They were creatures of habit, living out their golden years in the lap of luxury.

As a member of this bastion of Jewish pride, Roy would occasionally invite our tennis group to play on the well-tended clay courts of Hollywood. After a couple of hours of vigorous doubles, we would hang out for a little while just shooting the breeze. There was a guy in the group named Elliot who was a dentist with an erratic backhand and an acerbic wit. Initially I did not appreciate his wise comments, which just rubbed me the wrong way. It took a while, but I got used to him and eventually grew to like him quite a bit. Elliot had once been rejected for membership. Apparently, he had rubbed some other people the wrong way as well, and the question of membership was a sensitive topic for him.

Roy, who was president of the club at the time, pulled me aside and said, "Chuck, let's break Elliot's balls a little bit. Just go along with whatever I say."

I immediately agreed even without knowing where this was headed.

Roy then turned to me in front of everyone and said with a straight face, "Chuck, the Membership Committee is almost done with your application. It's looking pretty good."

I replied, "Roy, that's great. Thanks for all your help."

Elliot was not fooled for a second—he was well aware of my lack of standing in the community, both financially and socially. Without hesitation, he added, "Let me explain something to you guys. There are Nazis hiding out in Paraguay who have a better shot of becoming members of Hollywood than Chuck Levinsohn!" Everybody cracked up at that remark, but nobody laughed harder than me.

Elliot is gone now, but whenever I think of him, I remember that smartass comment, and it always makes me smile. That's not a bad legacy to leave behind.

CHAPTER FIFTEEN

THE NEXT BIG SCORE

WITH MO'S HELP, ROY AND I eventually landed a meeting with the managing partners of his law firm. We were purely on a fishing expedition, except this time we weren't on Mort's boat with roast beef sandwiches and Ballantine Ale. We were seated at a long table with a dozen of the most uptight-looking guys I had ever come across in my life. Roy looked very distinguished in his dark blue suit, perfectly knotted Windsor tie, and gray hair. I looked the part of a young gun whose job was to observe and keep his mouth shut.

Roy always had a low-key approach that served him well. He provided a brief introduction, making sure to use Mo's name several times. The body language of the partners loosened up once they realized they weren't going to be subjected to the usual boring sales pitch. Roy recognized which guy in the room had the most power and then got him to describe which benefits these lords and nobles already had in place. This stuff was a little over my head, but I followed along, feigning comprehension. Half smiles, slight nodding, and steady eye contact were the instinctive tools of a seasoned poker player.

They had every benefit under the sun, and I could tell that Roy was about to throw in the towel. Suddenly the leader of the pack blurted out, "Do you guys handle long-term care insurance? We have been considering looking into that." Without hesitation, Roy emphatically answered, "Sure, we work with that all the time."

I stared at him without breaking my frozen smile. Roy was bluffing. Our company didn't even carry that product!

The meeting reached its conclusion with the understanding that we would put together a cost/benefit analysis to provide to their benefits administrator. Fortunately, none of the lawyers had asked us any specific questions. That could have been awkward.

When we got into Roy's Mercedes to leave, we looked at each other and laughed. My suspicions were confirmed that he knew absolutely nothing about long-term care insurance. The division of labor was already clear to me. I would do all the work, and Roy would be the spokesperson, projecting the appearance of experience that only gray-haired guys in blue suits can exude. If we succeeded at this shot in the dark, we'd split the commissions fifty-fifty.

I became a quick study regarding something that I previously had no interest in and hadn't even been encouraged to sell. I found an outside brokerage firm that specialized in this coverage and developed a relationship with one of the owners. This was a big case, and she was naturally excited about helping land such a prestigious client. It was surreal that this former tobacco farmer would find himself at the epicenter of such a sophisticated business transaction. But I bore down on the materials necessary to form a cohesive proposal, examined offers from several insurance companies, and evaluated the pluses and minuses of each. I summarized my findings, articulating my recommendation in a letter addressed to the director of benefits at the law firm.

If I had studied this hard in college, I sure as hell wouldn't have been out hustling insurance. Maybe I would be on the Supreme Court by now, or CEO of a Fortune 500 company, or a famous author working on my latest novel. I might be living in comfort on a sprawling estate out in the country. I could just hop into my sports car and drive to Hollywood for a light lunch before a round of golf with some other big shots. Yeah, like that was ever happening!

All I knew was that if Roy and I pulled this off, we would be trailblazers in the wilderness of long-term care insurance. No one in our firm had ever sold it before, and we'd have done it with one of the blue-chip law firms in the state of New Jersey. Hail Roy and Chuck!

Not so fast. I had a proposal in hand, but I couldn't seem to make an appointment with Bruce, the firm's director of benefits. He had more pressing things to attend to, such as their annual health insurance renewal. What we were proposing was significant, but it paled in comparison to their health insurance coverage. Then I thought, *Maybe we can get a shot at that too!* I didn't know much about health insurance, but there were guys in our office a lot dumber than me cleaning up with selling that stuff.

I periodically wandered down to Roy's office to give him any updates that might arise. He had been doing this for years and knew that nothing is final until they sign on the dotted line. It's always that fucking dotted line, just sitting there, staring you down, daring you to seal the deal.

I didn't want to bother this guy Bruce, so I adopted a motto—"Be persistent without being a pest." Maxims like that sound good. Every couple of weeks, I gave him a call. He told me that we were on the agenda for their monthly management meeting, but every month we got canceled. I understood, this was a big firm. Our phone calls were always amiable, and I never sounded desperate even though I was.

In the blink of an eye, a year had come and gone since Roy and I had attended that initial meeting with the Twelve Wise Men. I had started thinking this might just end up being one of those pipe dreams that salesmen get all worked up about and then never materializes. We didn't bother Mo regarding this. He had done his part getting us in the door. I very rarely spoke to the broker who helped me in the beginning of this case. She had other fish to fry and had seen this movie before.

By virtue of my work with Roy, I was promoted out of a cubicle and into a small, windowless office. I was sitting there one morning just staring at the wall when the phone rang. It was Bruce, telling me they were ready to proceed. "What's the next step?" he asked. Caught off guard, I took a breath and gave a measured response conveying readiness and competence. I felt neither but couldn't let him know that.

So, the wheels were now in motion as I sprang into action. Papers were flying, phone lines were burning up, and there was excitement in the air. And all of this over an insurance policy to cover their executives in the event they happened to land in a nursing home in old age. Not the sexiest stuff in the world, but this was the business we'd chosen.

The proposal was carefully prepared and presented to Bruce. He quickly ratified it, and an appointment was set up to explain this rather dry subject to sixty attorneys. And I would be doing some of the explaining. I felt no fear about making this presentation to a room full of stiff suits, despite my complete lack of experience in this area. I would just be like an actor in a play, hoping I could remember my lines.

It would be a two-day meeting at their office with all the lawyers present. The woman from the brokerage firm would make the initial presentation, and then I would take it from there. There would be the obligatory question-and-answer period. I would resist the temptation to publicly confess that I had never sold this before and had crammed for this presentation like it was one of my college exams. Assuming I survived the Inquisition, they would be given short applications to fill out. This benefit would be paid for by the business and made available on a favorable basis to only the crème de la crème of the firm.

As I looked around the room at the faces of these entitled barristers, I felt no envy for their success. I knew by then that everything is a tradeoff. I could see in their eyes that they had their own problems. This seemed like a stressful environment, rife with expectations, stress, and petty jealousies. But for a twist of fate, this could have been me sitting among them.

As the process unfolded, my expertise grew every day. I oversaw this operation and moved the pieces around like they were on a chess board. Hey, I once tied a grandmaster at a chess exhibition in Israel. Of course, he was playing fifty people simultaneously, but I still tied him. I thought to myself, *This business stuff isn't that tough.* And then, *Don't get too cocky there, Bucko. "Pride cometh before the fall."*

It took about a month, and then the sale was complete. The lawyers had been approved by the insurance company, so Roy and I drove to their office to pick up the check for their annual premium. When I think about it now, it was kind of amazing. We didn't know anything at the beginning, and yet, first time out, sixty policies sold! Two weeks later, Roy and I were paid a healthy commission. This case took a year to get going, but once it began, it went smoothly. I developed good relations with my contacts at the law firm, and they even recommended us to several of the other big firms in New Jersey. I ended up making appointments at some of these outfits. These places were notorious for being difficult to even get in the door. Roy did not accompany me on any of these hunting trips, but we shared the commissions if I somehow bagged an elephant. That was the deal we'd made, and I honored it.

I grew into my role quickly as I sat in the conference rooms of the most prestigious law firms in the state. I was not full of myself but grateful that cutting tobacco, catching fish, and carrying lumber had given me the confidence to sit among these Masters of the Universe. I was now a long-term care insurance specialist. Go figure.

Other agents would come to me for help with their clients. If we made a sale, I would get paid and did not have to share any of this with Roy. After all, this wasn't the Mafia. I even became a public speaker on this topic, which had become a popular tool in retirement planning. I spoke to groups of tax accountants, senior clubs at churches, and elder care attorneys. After introducing myself, I would always tell the same joke to loosen up the crowd. "I graduated from college with a degree in philosophy. Imagine my parents' disappointment when they found out the Big Philosophy Companies weren't hiring!" I wasn't exactly Rodney Dangerfield, but I always got a laugh.

I was friendly with another agent, John, who set up a seminar for his large client base to generate interest in long-term care insurance. It took place in the conference room of a local nursing home. John's marketing director sent out fancy invitations advertising me as a nationally renowned long-term care speaker. There would be refreshments, literature, and a question-and-answer period. He received about two dozen RSVPs from people who would attend. I prepared twenty-four individual informative folders and drove about an hour to the facility. By the time I arrived, John's assistant had put out coffee, cranberry juice, and muffins for the crowd that would come rumbling in momentarily. I only hoped that we had enough seats available. We placed interest surveys on the table for the attendees to fill out to arrange individual appointments. The event was scheduled to begin at 4:00 p.m. At 3:45, nobody had yet arrived. At 4:00, still nobody had shown up. At 4:15, I was starting to get a bad feeling. At 4:30, we threw in the towel. A nationally renowned figure would be speaking, and not one person showed up. What the fuck! We packed up all the stuff and headed to the parking lot. That was twenty years ago. John and I still laugh about it to this day.

So many misadventures, so many high hopes, so much wasted time. That is the life of an insurance salesman. It's actually a good career, but for some reason I still can't believe that was really me. Sure, I wore those suits and monogrammed shirts and drove a Cadillac, but my true nature was back at DuroCraft. I stumbled blindly into the insurance business out of pure financial necessity. I faked it until I made it, and then when I made it, I was still faking it. That sounds like something Yogi Berra would say, but it makes sense to me.

CHAPTER SIXTEEN
A QUESTION OF BALANCE

L UCKILY FOR ME, I LIVED near the ocean. From the end of May to the beginning of October, I would carry my backpack and folding chair down to the local beach, late in the day after most of the people had gone home. That was the way I liked it. I got enough socialization at work and didn't need any here. I'd walk about twenty yards past the last person and claim my territory. With my chair, book, water, and iPod, I would be set for a couple of hours. I usually stayed until sundown and then walked home. I had already been doing this for years and have long been a firm believer in the positive effects of this pastime. They aren't quantifiable, but if you believe benefits exist, then they do. It's kind of like taking vitamins—you never really know for sure.

Evening sales appointments sometimes interfered with this routine, but that was okay. At this point, I was seeking balance in my life. I was making a decent living. Not a great one by other people's standards, but acceptable to mine. I was able to pay my bills, occasionally take women out to dinner, and play poker with my friends. And every month I put money into a retirement account just in case I lived to be old. I would never be rich—that would not be my destiny or even my goal. I just wanted to be independent, healthy, and peaceful. I desired a stress-free life as much as that is possible in this world. I would probably die trying.

The beach was an invaluable tool toward achieving that dream. I was criticized at work for coming and going as I pleased, but I didn't care. As long as I still produced, they couldn't do much. And my knowledge of long-term care had turned me into an undeniable asset to the firm. I continually led the agency in LTC sales and kept amassing more of those fake wooden plaques. In the end, collectible shit like that is meaningless, although for some reason I never threw them away.

After a couple of years, I traded in my Cadillac Eldorado for a used Lincoln Continental. At work it was referred to as the Mafia Staff Car. You don't see this car on the road anymore, mostly just in movies. Occasionally, you spot some ninety-year-old guy driving one of these relics down Ocean Avenue at about twenty miles an hour in the passing lane. He probably should no longer have a driver's license. I try not to think about it, but one day that could end up being me.

I purchased more suits and ties and custom shirts as my career demanded. Twenty years have blown by with me playing the role of an insurance salesman. As a result, I now possess a closet full of clothes that I will never wear again. That jammed-up closet has become a monument to an increasingly distant past. I wonder what becomes of all that stuff after you die. A lot of shit ends up in landfills, but those expensive suits and ties really need to find their way to a new home. It could be my only gift to humanity, donated by "Anonymous."

All the adventures from my previous life seem like an illusion to me now. I remember them, I talk about them, I write about them, but I feel disconnected from them as if I am writing about somebody else. I wish I had taken more photos from my time in Kentucky and Israel and California. We didn't have cell phones with cameras back then. I did have a Polaroid land camera that belonged to my father, but I only used it for my construction business. I took pictures of completed projects for my DuroCraft scrapbook, which I showed to prospective clients. I wish I had taken some group shots of that revolving door of misfits on my crew. That would have been a good idea, although not necessarily to show to potential customers. That might have spooked them from hiring us.

As time went by, I developed a better understanding of that group of old timers who met for lunch every day at Hollywood Country Club. They reminisced about everything from business ventures to romantic conquests. The veracity of their details was questionable, but it didn't matter. Those trips down memory lane kept them connected to their accomplishments. You preserve your identity like that. And essentially, that's what I'm doing here, preserving my identity.

I believe that everybody is a mixed bag of good and bad characteristics. Nobody is a perfect saint, and nobody is a perfect asshole. Maybe there are exceptions, especially in that latter category, but most personalities are like menus from Chinese restaurants—sweet and sour, one from Column A, one from Column B.

Outer appearances can be deceiving, because reflections in mirrors only scratch the surface. Outsiders define us by their own narrow standards. "What do you do for a living? Where do you live? Are you married? Do you have kids?" That line of questioning is legitimate, but it does not capture the true essence of a person. There is a rich inner life never revealed in superficial exchanges such as these.

It has been well documented that I did not fit the traditional mold of my upbringing. My mixed-bag theory should begin with me, the creator of the theory! Mine is an incongruous blend of peaceful habits offset by occasional waves of turmoil. My assets include high-minded pastimes such as writing, music, and long walks on the beach. My liabilities are marked by unstable finances, a fear of commitment, and a sense of isolation. When I lay it out like that, it seems like I am tilting in the wrong direction! It's a miracle that I've gotten this far without ever finding my true place in the world.

I have observed that as people grow older, their worst qualities often become more dominant. If someone has been abrasive in their youth, over time they become more so. If highly opinionated, it only gets worse. And if they're just plain argumentative, forget about it!

There are exceptions to *Levinsohn's Rules on Aging*. I know some formerly disgruntled souls who have mellowed with age. Their rough edges have been knocked off with the passing of time. These cases are rare but must be monitored for backsliding. You never know when they might suddenly snap back into a more disagreeable version of themselves.

Back on the beach, I do my best to fight off my worst tendencies from gaining a foothold. I admittedly can become misanthropic when provoked. My tolerance is routinely tested by the growing number of knuckleheads inhabiting this small planet.

I seek separation from their vibes when they threaten my peace of mind. I walk and breathe along the water's edge, creating a natural barrier—water on one side, air on the other. My strategy of asshole avoidance is not foolproof, especially when I'm jolted by the sudden laughter of hyenas in my midst. With a little time and distance, my equilibrium is usually restored. In the end, I'm just an imperfect man in an imperfect world. I take comfort in that knowledge.

From the beginning...

Going mobile

The old gang at our friend Jeff's Bar Mitzvah.
I'm looking over his shoulder, although
nobody seems to know what's going on!

The Big Day – May 25, 1963

The Voltaires, 1965

High school portrait, 1967

The Rebellion begins, 1970

Serenading my cousin at her wedding, 1974

Chilling out on the farm in Western Kentucky, 1975. Second row, but only my hair is visible!

Working on a fishing crew in Israel, 1977

The Levinsohn progression
upper left – 4th generation in America, me
lower left – Murray, my father
upper right – Abraham, my great-grandfather
lower right – Charles, my grandfather

Ancestors gathered in Vilna, Lithuania, circa 1890

CHAPTER SEVENTEEN
FATSO

TURNING FIFTY CAME UP ON me fast. The year was 2000—the millenium! It seemed like only yesterday that I was lean and tan and sweating in the fields of Kentucky at twenty-five years old. And my muscles were sinewy and rippled as I hauled in heavy nets of fish on the Mediterranean coast before I was even thirty. And my shoulders were broad as I lifted massive wooden girders on Jersey construction sites at thirty-five. Those were glorious days when I was still young and strong.

But times had changed. I now devoured huge lunches with a bunch of guys in suits every day. I exercised less. And at night, I went out and sat at the bar of a local pub, drinking Scotch and eating prime rib dinners. Then I drove home and fell asleep in my reclining chair.

One weekend, a female friend invited me to attend a Bar Mitzvah with her. The photographer walked around taking group pictures of each table, and later, the host mailed them out to everybody. I didn't see myself in the picture. I saw the woman whom I had accompanied, but who was that next to her? Holy shit! It was me. I was all swollen up! I looked like Jerry Lewis when he was on steroids. So, I went and bought a scale. It read 235 pounds! How was that possible? Sure, every time I'd bought a new pair of pants, I needed a bigger size. I guess that 42-inch waist should have tipped me off that something was wrong.

When guys go to department stores shopping for pants, there are certain benchmarks at play. When you're young, almost everybody wears a size 28 waist. That's standard. Only freaks maintain that throughout their lives. As time goes on, you creep up through a progression—30, 32, 34, and then 36. A 36-inch waist is kind of the outer edge of the trouser universe. After that, it's uncharted territory. Fewer options, distorted dressing-room mirrors, and lowered self-esteem are just some of the side effects. You go through several stages of grief, and then things only get worse—38, 40, and then you have entered the Twilight Zone. A 42-inch waist means you have failed. You are weak, stupid, and a slave to your appetites!

I had let myself go to pot and didn't even realize it. Suddenly I was being bombarded with
comments about my appearance. I ran into my
friend's Uncle Sol in the supermarket. He said,
"Hey, Chollie, what's with all the weight?" Sol had
been my insurance agent when I was in the construction business. He was an old school Jew with
a thick Brooklyn accent. He was one of the most
memorable characters I have ever known, and his
opinion meant a lot to me.

A few days later, some other guy I knew walked
up to me at the local deli. I was sitting there mind-
ing my own business, reading the newspaper, and
eating a corned beef sandwich. "Hey, Chucky, what
happened to you?" And this guy was a fat slob! I
would see him at the beach club with his bald head
and big hairy belly. And now even this guy was
giving me shit?

Enough was enough. I raised myself up and
shouted from the mountain top, "This will not
stand! Things are gonna change!" But how? I had
never been on a diet in my life. The thought of
dieting sounded terrible and foreign to me. But I
had no choice. This skinny Jewish kid was now a
middle-aged fatso.

I threw out the Breyer's ice cream and
Entenmann's chocolate chip cookies that were
steady staples in my apartment. You know those
cookies. They're soft and sweet, and you can't stop

eating them! Instead, I went out and bought cottage cheese. Ugh! Cottage cheese—the symbolic food of personal failure. Only losers eat cottage cheese.

I then stumbled onto a technique that I could stay with. I would just eat less. Genius! I still went to lunch with the guys, but I wouldn't finish my food. I ate half my sandwich and a few french fries and then placed my napkin over the plate. *Finito!* My meal was officially done. Push the plate far away to discourage the temptation to reach back for more. Treat every single meal like this. Reduce my Scotch intake. Increase my water consumption. Join a gym. Walk more on the Boardwalk. Add up all these healthy habits and over time, I would no longer resemble that fat fuck Jerry Lewis! Nothing personal, Jerry. I know he was sick and had to take steroids as part of his treatment. At least he had an excuse. I'd gotten this way all on my own!

I flipped the switch and reached deep into the well of my character. I located my lost sense of discipline and applied it to this new regimen. I did not waver and did not look back. I was committed to losing this unacceptable weight, step by step, one pound at a time. *Damn, if I had applied this kind of commitment to my career, I'd be retired by now!*

Amazingly, this approach began to work even faster than I'd imagined. This was not a great hardship for me. This was moderation, not deprivation. I had watched friends become miserable by the restrictions of commercial diets that they paid good money for. Their sense of frustration was written all over their faces as they struggled to show any progress for their extreme efforts. When they finally did achieve their goals, they went out and bought new wardrobes to celebrate. Invariably, that sense of exultation was short-lived. The way they got there was not sustainable, and they eventually had to retrieve their old wardrobes featuring larger sizes. I was no expert, but it seemed that the world of dieting was a scam, a vicious cycle of success and backsliding built for profit on the backs of vanity.

In less than two months, I had dropped about twenty pounds with my program of reduced intake and increased exercise. I lost another ten pounds in a manner that I don't recommend. I was at my poker game and forced to leave early due to acute pain in my side. I ended up in the emergency room of the hospital with a kidney stone. I underwent surgery and spent about a week there. Besides getting rid of that painful stone, an unintended benefit was this additional weight loss. I was sure that I would gain those ten pounds back, but I never did.

I eventually got down to just over 200 pounds. I was proud of my effort, but I knew that if I didn't remain vigilant, it could all be for naught. Going forward, I continued to maintain a lifestyle of moderation versus deprivation. Now twenty years later, my fighting weight is a svelte 185 pounds! It's hard to believe that I once weighed fifty pounds more than this. I was lucky I saw that embarrassing photo of myself when I did. Who knows what would have happened if I had continued down the path of unimpeded weight gain? For someone who claims he never caught a break, I caught a big one that time. It probably saved my life.

CHAPTER EIGHTEEN

IT WAS A GOOD RUN

IT WAS DURING THIS TIME that my mother passed away. Lil was eighty-seven and had outlived my father by twenty-eight years. She had gotten remarried again when she was seventy-three. Her third husband, Bill, died about eight years after they got married.

I was at work when I got a call from my mother's housekeeper. She had found Lil lying on the floor unconscious. She was taken by ambulance to the emergency room. She had an aneurysm with no expectation of recovery. After a while, she was moved to a semiprivate room. I called my sister in Boston. She and my brother-in-law hopped in their car for the five-hour drive to New Jersey.

I sat in that hospital room as my mother lay in bed unconscious, with nothing to do but wait. It was only a matter of time. My father's death had been tragic because at fifty-nine, he was still a young man. My mother's demise was sudden but not tragic. She had been married three times, losing all three husbands. She had children, grandchildren, and great-grandchildren. She had more friends than I could count. She had lived in nice homes and had maids who prepared her meals. She had enjoyed nice vacations and belonged to beach clubs and organizations. Although she was somewhat of a hypochondriac, she had been healthy for most of her life. All in all, it had been a good run.

After I had been sitting there for many hours, a few of my friends came by to visit. Then the nurse walked in and looked at the monitor by the bed. It had flat-lined. She turned to me and said, "I'm sorry, she's gone." I walked out into the hallway to let it sink in, then saw my sister and brother-in-law coming off the elevator. They'd missed seeing her alive one last time by just a few minutes.

After the dust settled and arrangements were made and condolences were paid, it hit us that our mother was really gone. My sister, Jackie, made a good observation. "Lil gave us a great gift. She died painlessly in one day without being sick. If she'd landed in a nursing home for an extended period of time, it would've been a nightmare for her and for us."

My mother was a real piece of work—she was the original mixed bag. She could be loving and affectionate one minute and then turn on a dime the next. Suddenly you'd find yourself on the receiving end of her infamous cold shoulder. She played the Jewish guilt card as if she'd invented it. As a kid, I was too young to understand why she said the things she did. I think now that she felt sorry for herself because of some personal losses suffered earlier in life, but I really don't know.

Later, her greatest love became gambling. This was unfortunate, since she usually had no money. When she did, she would beg me to drive her to Atlantic City so she could play slot machines for a couple of hours. When Bill was still alive, I would occasionally drive the two of them down there. Bill would watch me shoot craps for a while—this was during a stretch of time when I was a steady winner. Then he and I would go to the cocktail lounge for drinks, while Lil played her machines. She'd come find us when she was done. I could tell in a second by her demeanor whether she had won or lost. She never quite grasped the concept of quitting while you're ahead.

I used to go to her beach club occasionally as a guest. I liked some of the people there, but I didn't care for all the commotion around the pool area. If I arrived early, I'd grab a lounge chair and towel and head down the beach to the water's edge. I'd dive into the Atlantic Ocean and body surf in the clear cool waves that would be rolling in. Afterward, I'd climb out of the water and lay down on my beach chair. I'd let the sun's hot rays dry me off. I felt peaceful and refreshed. I would just start dozing off when suddenly I'd hear a voice calling, "Chuck, Chuck!" Squinting through the sunlight, I'd see Lil standing up on the deck. She'd be waving for me to come up. I'd begrudgingly trudge up the sandy hill. She'd smile and say, "I wanted to let you know that I was here." I thought to myself, "Really? That's what you wanted to tell me?" I'd reply, "Okay, good, well I'm going back down to the beach now." She'd add, "I'll be playing cards with my friends if you need me." I'd kiss her on the cheek and walk slowly back to the water's edge, knowing I had no shot at falling asleep again.

As far back as I can remember, Lil and I were never on the same page. She could be exasperating, and I could be impatient. When she would call me on the phone, I would have to hold the receiver away from my ear. She just kept talking and changing topics seamlessly in a one-way conversation. I would check in periodically just in case she asked me a question. I wasn't the best son, but I wasn't the worst either. My only real regret is that my father didn't live long enough for them to spend their golden years together.

After she died that night in the hospital, I went home and lay in bed staring at the light in the window. It felt surreal that she was gone from this world. I lay there awake for quite a while, just staring, not really thinking. Irrevocable losses in life happen to everyone, but when they happen to you, it takes time for it to sink in. For some people, it never does.

CHAPTER NINETEEN

THE LIFE OF A GAMBLER

After a parent passes away, you tend to take stock of your own situation. In my case, I had finally attained my goal of creating a balanced lifestyle. I had a respectable job, a healthy exercise routine, an active social life, and time to relax on the beach. Okay, so maybe I wasn't exactly a Renaissance Man, but at least I was diversified.

By then, I had been playing poker for close to twenty years and was part of a group of guys who played in local games during the week. Every Monday, Wednesday, and Friday we got together at somebody's house for an evening of cards. This was not for small money. It was enough money, in fact, to provide supplemental income to the steady winners. And accordingly, there were always steady losers. Those guys generally had bad habits and made no effort to improve. They could get lucky on any given night, but when the dust settled at the end of the year, they were deep in the red. I'd been in a lot of different games and noticed that consistent losers all had one thing in common—they never folded. They were either cockeyed optimists or just afraid of being bluffed out. Either way, they wouldn't give up a hand. The results were usually disastrous. They might curse and throw the cards and claim they hated poker, but a minute later they'd ask, "Are we still playing on Friday?" These losers just loved to play—or maybe they just wanted time away from their wives. I don't really know, but come Friday, they'd be in their seats raring to go!

John was the house man for the Wednesday night game and provided a generous spread of Italian food, coffee, cake, and ice cream. He recouped the cost of the food by "chopping the pot." He removed a red $5 chip from every pot all night long. Running a home poker game was a profitable venture except on the nights when John lost and blew the whole chop back. Then the tirade would begin. He'd blame the cards, he'd blame the guys, he'd blame everything but his own poor play. And like clockwork, he would bitterly announce that he hated poker. Then he'd add, "I must've run over a nun today." I didn't know what that meant, but got that it can't be good. Everybody laughed, and he would tell us to go fuck ourselves. And then he would deal another hand.

John's Wednesday night game has lasted for decades. There's an occasional turnover of players as guys go broke, move away, or, in some cases, even die. I have been to a number of wakes for deceased poker players, with undoubtedly more to come. After all, we're not getting any younger.

I liked most of the guys in these games, although there was always one or two who got on my nerves. Granted, I may not have been the most tolerant person in the world, but objectively speaking, some people are just plain assholes. And this truism isn't limited only to the poker world, although it is magnified there. Think about it. You're sitting around a table with ten guys for eight hours fighting for each other's hard-earned money. There were always a lot of stupid comments flying around. I mean this wasn't exactly a Mensa society meeting. My problem was that I let all the bullshit bother me. I might overreact to a remark leading to an exchange of insults, which might be followed by an extended period of bad vibes. Given the stakes involved, these types of incidents were common and not just limited to me. Amazingly, in the history of this game, there were never any acts of violence.

I was taking this enterprise seriously, so I read every book on poker that I could get my hands on, determined to improve my game any way I could. I bought *Super Systems* by Doyle Brunson. This was the Bible of poker books—600 pages of wisdom written by the Godfather himself. Doyle "Texas Dolly" Brunson was a World Series champion and an old school gambler. He made his bones as a young man in West Texas in the early '60s. He and his pals drove all over the Southwest looking for easy card games, often sleeping in their cars, winning big, going broke, and starting over again. Doyle Brunson, Johnny Moss, Amarillo Slim, and Benny Binion were pioneers who could've lived in the 1800s. These men were ageless figures the likes of whom will not be seen again. The last three are all gone, but Doyle remains. He was a beloved figure in a diverse poker community populated by both noblemen and creeps. He's an old man now, but "Texas Dolly" is still the legend. He may walk with a cane, but when he enters the room, everything stops. (I should note that since the original time of this writing, Doyle Brunson has sadly passed away in May of 2023.)

I was now studying game strategy while working to eliminate my kryptonite—my volatile temperament at the table. I was making progress on both fronts. Now when guys were spouting nonsense, I became like a jujitsu master turning their inattention against them while I remained focused. I was there to win and not to fuck around. These were mostly rich guys, and I was not. I remained amiable on the outside, but inside, I was treating it like a business. I even resuscitated my old ledger to record my increasingly positive results.

I only played good starting cards, so I folded more often. I bluffed rarely but effectively, and I kept my cool. I played in home games during the week and drove to Atlantic City on the weekends. I usually played at the Trump Taj Mahal. The Taj had the biggest and best poker room on the East Coast. They even shot a scene there for the movie *Rounders*, starring Matt Damon and Edward Norton. I got a Taj Player's Club Card, which entitled me to free rooms and free meals. The more hours I played, the more perks I received. Looking back, I'm amazed that I had time for anything else, yet I still managed to work and maintain a social life. Granted both of those areas suffered, but not catastrophically. Not yet anyway.

When the United States Poker Tournament came to the Taj, I signed up for several events. I was able to get a free room for a week, so I took off from work and adopted the lifestyle of a full-time gambler. The poker world struck me as a low culture inhabited by an unsavory mix of characters. There were some well-respected players who made a living from it, but there was always a full contingent of lowlifes, street hustlers, and wannabes. This scene basically ran the full gamut of human experience. Existing on the edge of this environment, I tried to create a barrier to separate myself from the general population. Wearing sunglasses, a baseball hat, and listening to my iPod were the props I used to keep my distance.

It was hard to believe that I once worked on a kibbutz in Israel, embracing the health and fresh air of the Mediterranean Sea. What a contrast to this! When the tournament was on a break, I walked out on the Boardwalk and breathed in the salty air of the Atlantic. It wasn't quite the same, but it helped renew me at least until the next break.

Over time, I became familiar with the players who followed these tournaments around. They all knew each other and existed in kind of an unholy fraternity. I never broke into their ranks, keeping mostly to myself. I observed their little cliques and how they behaved. I found their freewheeling lifestyle appealing up to a point, but something just seemed off—their rebellion against traditional norms felt unsustainable to me.

At first, I had limited success in these tournaments, but I progressed quickly. I incorporated a more nuanced strategy, which was the difference between getting eliminated and getting paid. Of course, there was always the unpredictable factor of luck, but that exists in every aspect of life. It can make you or break you. Sadly, a talented person without luck is a tragic figure.

I was over fifty years old, and my previously balanced life had become tilted in one direction. I was playing cards three nights during the week, plus every weekend. It was understandably difficult to maintain a girlfriend during this time. There were some attractive women who played in the card-room, but they were not good candidates for a relationship. They were even more obsessed with poker than most guys. I did meet some ladies back home who were not totally horrified by my lifestyle. A couple of them may have even thought it was cool. You know, the kind of women who are attracted to outlaws. I may have been different from the guys they usually dated, but I was hardly an outlaw.

It had been twenty years since my introduction to Atlantic City and ten years since my failed attempt to move to Las Vegas. As I would glide down the steep escalator from the parking garage to the lobby of the Trump Taj Mahal, I felt like I was floating on air. There's a scene in *Rounders* when Matt Damon and Edward Norton are coming down that same escalator. Their acting perfectly captures the anticipation you feel as you slowly descend onto the plush purple and gold carpeting of the casino floor. I didn't judge myself for these life choices one way or the other—this was just what was happening. From my journey as a songwriter to a tobacco farmer, fisherman, carpenter, and salesman, this was where the road had led me.

I'm not sure if you can call it evolution or maybe it's the opposite—I don't really know. Like always, I just wanted to be the best that I could be at every endeavor. I couldn't say for sure if my late father would be proud of the unconventional man I had become. Those types of thoughts linger with you for a lifetime. I wonder about it still.

CHAPTER TWENTY
THE THREE AMIGOS

I T WAS DURING THIS TIME that I began going on annual vacations to Las Vegas with the Three Amigos—Big Tony, Steve Pizza, and John. We were the Jersey Boys, comprised of three Italians and one Jew. I was like the Meyer Lansky of the group. Well, maybe not exactly. Meyer Lansky was the financial wizard behind the Italian Mafia, and I was clearly no wizard, financial or otherwise.

The son of Russian immigrants, Meyer Lansky grew up on the Lower East Side with Bugsy Siegel and Lucky Luciano. They worked their way up from the streets, eventually forming the largest organized crime syndicate in the United States. Meyer supplied the brain power for their nefarious schemes, while the others supplied the muscle. The creation of Las Vegas as we know it is a result of their collaboration. The character of Hyman Roth in *The Godfather Part 2* was based on Meyer Lansky. I once made a list of my ten favorite people of all time. For some inexplicable reason, I also included Meyer Lansky among the filmmakers, musicians, and do-gooders who had made it into my vaunted list.

Once again, I had professed admiration for the rebellious nature of outlaws, gangsters, and gamblers. With that questionable choice of role models, I was lucky that I never became an arch criminal myself! In truth, it was never a remote possibility. My Jewish middle-class upbringing always protected me from ever drifting too far to the dark side.

Although I grew up with many Italian friends, hanging out with the Three Amigos for an entire week required courage and fortitude. For six years in a row, we stayed at different casino resorts on the Vegas Strip. It was a long flight from Newark Airport, but the excitement of landing in Vegas always superseded travel fatigue. We'd check into our hotel rooms, change our watches to the new time zone, and get right into the swing of things. I tried to pace myself, knowing we had a whole week ahead of us.

In the mornings, we met for a massive breakfast at the buffet. It's well documented how much I've always loved a breakfast buffet! Sufficiently fueled up for the day, we'd usually spend the afternoon at the pool, relaxing and admiring the bathing beauties who were virtually everywhere. Las Vegas is a magnet for that.

Occasionally we'd walk down the Strip, exploring such architectural masterpieces as The Mirage, Mandalay Bay, Paris, and Caesars Palace. This town is possibly the most stimuli-laden destination on Earth. Sometimes we rented a car for the day and drove to the Hoover Dam, Red Rock Canyon, or Lake Mead. It was good to do some sightseeing away from the city. Even the Three Amigos needed an occasional break from nonstop gambling, eating, and drinking.

In the evenings, we dined at one of the fine restaurants in our hotel. If we'd gambled enough, we'd get comped for those meals. Occasionally, we visited one of the many strip clubs that Vegas is famous for. These clubs were a lot different from the local go-go bars back home. As the gambling capital of the world, the owners knew all their customers had loads of cash on them and their goal was to extract as much of it as possible. Gorgeous women from all over the country flew into Vegas for the weekend to work in the upscale clubs. These glitzy palaces all had soft leather couches where you sat and relaxed and ordered overpriced drinks. Within minutes, shapely girls of all nationalities would come up and sit next to you. They pressed their legs against you and looked into your eyes and smiled. They stroked your shoulder and asked you your name and where you were from. They nodded amiably, exuding genuine interest in your answers. They had no problem convincing some middle-aged guys on vacation to pay $20 for a lap dance to a three-minute song. One dance was generally not enough. With each passing song, the dancers became a little more intimate. The customers slowly loosened up from the alcohol, perfume, and soft bodies pressing against them and any sense of the value of money flew out the window. Generous tips flowed like wine.

The owners got a piece of everything the girls made apart from their tips. It's a brilliant business model that succeeds all over the world, essentially cashing in on human desire and moral weakness. It's not really as decadent as it sounds, although that cannot be said of the seedier spots on the backstreets of Sin City. In those dark places, everything is for sale. It's a good thing we didn't have clubs like that back home or a lot of guys would've gone broke.

After dinner, we'd get down to the more serious business of gambling. Two of the Three Amigos were blackjack players. I was not. I always sought out a poker game, usually at The Mirage or the Bellagio where I might even spot Doyle Brunson and other poker luminaries. The Bellagio has a special room reserved for high rollers where someone could win or lose $100,000 in a single session. To me, these high-stake gamblers existed in another universe far, far away.

On our first trip there in 1998, Big Tony somehow wangled tickets for us to see Siegfried and Roy at The Mirage. This was the hottest act in Vegas, and they had been playing at The Mirage for over a decade. They were originally magicians and illusionists from Germany, but over time, they had also become world-class animal trainers and incorporated beautiful lions, leopards, and tigers into their extravagant act. These once ferocious animals would be on stage maybe only twenty yards away from the audience. Siegfried and Roy could miraculously make them vanish into thin air right in front of your eyes. It was an incredible production, hence its staying power in the entertainment capital of the world.

During a live show in 2003, Roy was mauled and dragged offstage by Montecore, a 400-pound Siberian tiger. Something had spooked him, and this had never happened before. Roy survived massive injuries and multiple surgeries, but their long-standing engagement at The Mirage came to an unfortunate end.

On that same trip, Big Tony invited his business partner's daughter, who had been living there for several years, to dinner. We met her at the Palm Steak House in Caesars Palace, a famous restaurant often frequented by celebrities. We recognized the mayor of Las Vegas, Oscar Goodman, who had appeared in the Martin Scorsese movie, *Casino*. I was going to order a porterhouse steak but then a waiter walked by carrying a tray with a huge lobster on it. I was sitting next to John and said, "Did you see that?"

"Yeah, that looked pretty good."

"I'm think I'm getting that."

"Yeah, me too."

The waiter came to take our order, and we all started with shrimp cocktails, chopped salad, and warm rolls. For entrées, the others ordered steaks or lamb chops with sides of potatoes and creamed spinach. When the waiter got to me and John, we asked, "How big are those lobsters?"

"Three pounds and stuffed with crab meat!"

We practically said in unison, "I'll have that!"

The waiter replied, "Good choice, gentlemen."

Nobody bothered to ask how much it cost.

We all ate like kings that night. We topped it all off with espresso, gelato, pastries, and sambuca. What a meal! Then the waiter brought the check in a leather binder. Big Tony reached for it and looked at it, then shouted his standard line, "Ho! What, did we break furniture here?" I have no idea how much the bill was. We found out later that those lobsters cost $120 each! Since this dinner was Big Tony's idea, we just assumed he was paying for it, and he could afford it. After all, he had gotten rich in the construction business on the backs of working stiffs like me! So, he took out his American Express business card and graciously paid the bill.

The week came to an end, and we waited in the airport for our flight home. It was time to settle up for the airline tickets, limos, and show tickets. Big Tony had laid out the money for all those items on his credit card, but we had paid for our hotel rooms separately. He informed us, "You guys each owe me $550 for the plane tickets, $150 for the limo, and $100 for the tickets to the show." Okay, that sounded right. We all reached for our cash to pay up. Then he said, "Hold it," and looked at me and John. "I was gonna pay for that dinner at the Palm until you two assholes ordered those lobsters! Now all three of you owe me another $120!"

Steve threw up his hands up in protest. "But I didn't order a lobster!"

Big Tony dismissed him like he was swatting away a fly. "Take it up with those nitwit friends of yours," he said, pointing at me and John.

We all cracked up. Big Tony was no Don Rickles, but his brand of insult humor was still very good.

These Vegas vacations provided a timeless highlight reel of gambling, sightseeing, great food, and uproarious laughter. With the Three Amigos, there was never a dull moment. Jersey-style ball-breaking apparently could cross state lines without missing a beat. Anthony and John were the main perpetrators, with Steve as their primary target. I was merely an innocent Jew along for the ride. Win, lose, or draw, these trips were always memorable and our Vegas adventures would be recounted for years to come. They also laid the groundwork for what would become my next big solo undertaking.

CHAPTER TWENTY-ONE
THE WSOP

IT WAS AROUND THE YEAR 2000 that poker exploded onto the national stage. Televised events were everywhere. Movie stars and athletes competed against professional players who suddenly became household names. Poker magazines were sold in drug stores and supermarkets. Books on strategy filled up the shelves at Barnes and Noble stores. They even broadcast a special poker tournament on TV just before the Super Bowl!

And then internet poker burst onto the scene. You could fund an account on your computer with sites like Party Poker or Poker Stars and play all day from the comfort of home in your bathrobe. This phenomenon spread like wildfire. A lot of people became addicted. I caught a break—I didn't like it. It gave me a headache.

I had a new goal anyway, having decided to fly out to Vegas to compete in the 2004 World Series of Poker. I was fifty-four, and this would be the latest in a long line of impulsive moves for me. None of my other friends who played cards would do something like this. I'm not exactly sure why. I was not what we called a "sick gambler." We all knew people like that, and it was an illness—the compulsion, lack of control, the self-destructive tendencies. Fortunately, I did not suffer from that, much in the same way that I did not suffer from alcoholism. I liked to sit at a bar and sip two Scotches before dinner, but that did not make me an alcoholic. I definitely had some bad habits, but I did not have addictions. I may have been excessive in all things in my youth, but less so as I got older. I think I caught a break in that regard.

When I was growing up, a lot of guys liked to gamble. Monmouth Park Racetrack was only a couple of miles away. As teenagers, we would sneak in after school and bet on horses. Horse racing is very exciting, and some of the guys maintained a deep interest in that sport for the rest of their lives.

Almost everybody loved to bet on football games back then. When we got older, we'd place the bets with bookies. I sensed the danger of that activity, not because you'd get your legs broken like in the movies but because you had an endless line of credit. You could easily get in over your head, and many guys would try to bet their way out of a hole on Monday that they'd dug on Sunday. That was generally a recipe for disaster.

We used to have a ritual on Sunday mornings. We'd go over to Rich's apartment and have bagels and lox and coffee and study the newspapers and make our picks. We'd place our bets and then watch the games. You'd live and die with every play. Guys would be screaming at the TV. It was just too manic, too unhealthy. Like all gambling, it was only fun when you won.

Sometimes on Saturdays, I'd go over to Big Tony's house to bet and watch the college games. He was one of the few successful sports bettors I knew, in part because he was a contrarian. It took guts to go against the grain, but he could do it. When everybody else was losing, Big Tony was winning. Eventually though, even his luck ran out.

Sports betting is a tough racket. Most guys get a little taste of success, but then the odds catch up with them and they're forced to surrender. Only sick gamblers chase their money until there's nothing left.

I had settled on poker where I would be a participant rather than a handicapper. Over time, my experience and studying paid off and I became a solid winning player. Imagine if I had applied that laser-like discipline to my college studies and career! There's no telling what I might've achieved. I used to think about that a lot, but as Austin Powers mused, "That train sailed a long time ago."

Those considerations notwithstanding, I bought a round-trip plane ticket from Newark to Vegas, booked a hotel room for a week, and ordered a limo to the airport. If I were going to do this, I would do it up right.

The World Series of Poker began in 1970, the acronym quickly becoming the WSOP. It was the brainchild of Benny Binion, who owned the Horseshoe Hotel and Casino in downtown Las Vegas. He was born in West Texas in 1904 and had turned to a life of crime early on. He began as a bootlegger, bookie, and loan shark, and eventually ran illegal gambling in Dallas. Balls and brains got him to the top, but violence and corruption kept him there. In 1931, he was convicted of murdering a black numbers runner. Texas was a very racist state back then, and Benny was well-connected, so prejudice and political payoffs saved him from the inconvenience of incarceration. He received a two-year suspended sentence. Despite numerous scuffles with the law, Benny continued to climb up the criminal food chain. Things changed in 1950 when the Chicago Outfit moved in on his operation. Benny fled for his life, leaving Texas and relocating to Las Vegas, just one more shady character seeking a fresh start in the desert sands of southern Nevada.

He acquired two beat-up hotels in downtown Las Vegas and combined them into one upscale property. Binion's Horseshoe Casino quickly became a popular destination for high-stakes gamblers and hoods. "Good food, good whiskey cheap, and a good gamble," was Benny's business motto. His sins from Texas were washed away, and like Moe Daelitz, he became another venerable citizen in Glitter Gulch. That was until 1953, when he was sentenced to five years in Leavenworth penitentiary for tax evasion. He served forty-two months. They revoked his gambling license, but his family still operated the Horseshoe, with Benny calling the shots from prison.

Time went by and Las Vegas grew by leaps and bounds, and Benny's footprint grew with it. In 1970, he invented the World Series of Poker. He invited seven players to compete, including Doyle Brunson, Johnny Moss, and Amarillo Slim. Johnny Moss, at age sixty-three, was declared the first World Champion. Every year, the field of players increased, with Amarillo Slim winning it once and Doyle Brunson winning twice. The tournament continued to grow exponentially. The WSOP stayed at the Horseshoe for more than thirty years. Benny eventually lost his gambling license permanently. His oldest son, Jack, who was highly respected in the community, ran the WSOP successfully for many years thereafter. On the other hand, Benny's younger son, Ted, was repeatedly busted for drug offenses and for consorting with a Chicago mobster, Herbert "Fat Herbie" Blitzstein, but his family connections succeeded in keeping him out of prison.

In 1998, Ted Binion was kidnapped, held for ransom, and then murdered by his ex-stripper girlfriend and her lover. The trial was a media circus, and the family name was dragged through the mud. The Horseshoe soon fell on hard times and was eventually sold at a discount to Harrah's Entertainment.

Benny Binion died in 1989 at the age of eighty-five. Despite a life of violence, crime, and incarceration, he managed to carve out a niche of respectability in the only place on Earth that could be possible. He was elected posthumously to the Poker Hall of Fame, not as a player but as a visionary. I'm amazed there hasn't been a major motion picture made about his life and times.

By the time I arrived in 2004, the WSOP was being held at the Rio, a few blocks off the Las Vegas Strip. The WSOP had grown to include more than thirty different events with various entry fees. The Main Event was always No-Limit Texas Hold 'Em with a $10,000 fee and a first place prize of a million dollars. ESPN would broadcast the final table live on national TV. That was clearly way over my head, so I registered for a $1,500 event featuring my favorite poker game, Omaha Hi-Lo. I already knew this game inside and out but wanted to fine tune my skills ahead of the tournament, so for a week before my trip, I plunged headfirst into a basic training course with the dedication of a Navy SEAL. I studied Doyle Brunson's chapter on Omaha Hi-Lo in *Super Systems* and applied that knowledge to warm-up tournaments on Party Poker. By the time my limo picked me up, I was an Omaha Hi-Lo killing machine, supremely confident in my ability to crush the competition.

I checked into my room at the Aladdin Hotel and rented a car to drive back and forth at will. It was the middle of June and 110 degrees outside. After the long flight, I really needed to relax. My body was stiff, and I just wanted to go float in the hotel pool and let the tightness in my back and neck unwind. But it was so hot out that you literally couldn't hang out at the pool—dry heat, my ass! In retrospect, I felt my experience for that entire week was somehow hampered by that initial discomfort. After all my preparation, I think it might have set me off on the wrong foot.

The tournament started the next day and would last for as long as needed, depending on the participation. About 360 players put up $1,500 each, with the final 36 players receiving incrementally increasing payouts. First prize was approximately $150,000. With ten years under my belt in the insurance business, I had built up a bankroll, but winning this event would be life-changing. My mantra for this tournament was "Dare to dream." Actually, I would've been happy to just finish in the top thirty-six. That would've been validation enough for all my efforts during this rather unorthodox phase of my life.

The Rio was a huge casino hotel owned by Harrah's Entertainment and had this corny Carnival theme throughout the resort. The tournament was held in a spacious convention hall called the Amazon Room. The funny thing was that as brutally hot as it was outside, it was equally cold inside. The fucking Amazon Room was like a walk-in freezer! I had to go to the gift shop and buy a sweatshirt just to keep from shivering. At the end of the day, when I would walk out to the parking lot to my rental car, it was like I was suddenly thrust onto the surface of the sun. Within five seconds, I'd experienced a sixty-degree temperature swing!

"Shuffle up and deal!" The classic announcement kicking off the action bellowed through the tournament director's microphone. Here I was in Las Vegas playing in the World Series of Poker! The room was jammed as a few other tournaments were going on simultaneously. I spotted several well-known players in the room whom I recognized from TV. I must admit, the whole vibe was pretty exciting. Scantily clad girls in tank tops and shorts were walking around promoting products for various sponsors. It was kind of a distraction as I tried to settle into my maximum concentration mode. I was used to playing in tournaments in Atlantic City, but they were nothing in comparison to the circus atmosphere of this scene.

Once the cards were dealt, the initial jitters disappeared. I tuned out all the distractions and attempted to play perfect poker, start to finish. A lot of people seemed to know each other, probably from playing regularly on the tournament circuit. They were very chatty at the table as if they were in a home game. I didn't know a soul, so I just kept to myself. I listened to some music on my iPod and tried to concentrate on each hand. Unfortunately, my body still felt uptight, and I kept shifting around, trying to get comfortable.

This was a slow-moving tournament, scheduled to last about twelve hours on the first day and then conclude the next day. Hunched over a chair, staring at cards with a bad back for twelve hours would become a test of endurance. Hey, Doyle Brunson was more than twenty years older than me, and he could do it! Of course, he'd been doing this his whole life. Back in the day on those West Texas road trips, they sometimes played for thirty-six hours straight.

Despite everything, I was playing well. I made no mistakes. Because of the luck factor, you could play a hand perfectly against a bad player and still lose the hand. Psychologically, you had to take these setbacks in stride. I'd see guys who were obviously terrible players accumulate mountains of chips early in the tournament. Being philosophical, I knew that if I could just survive, those chips would eventually be redistributed and hopefully in my direction.

I made it to the second day, which was no small feat. I drove back to the Aladdin and had dinner and a shower and went to bed. I was back at the Rio the next morning, feeling refreshed. The session wore on and soon players were being eliminated steadily. My play was consistent and disciplined, but I hit a bad stretch of luck at an inopportune time. My chips began to evaporate, and it wasn't long before I was eliminated from the tournament. I finished 120th out of 360 players, far from the payouts. Not terrible, but not the validation I'd sought. I took the high road and embraced it as a learning experience, then treated the remainder of the week as a vacation, eating, drinking, and gambling. I flew back to Jersey in decent spirits with every intention of returning the following year.

CHAPTER TWENTY-TWO

THE WSOP PART TWO

A ND RETURN I DID FOR the 2005 WSOP. I'd amazingly had a good year at work, and this time I signed up for the $3,000 Omaha Hi-Lo tournament. Four hundred players posted their entry fees, with first place winning approximately $300,000! Once again, the top thirty-six players would receive prize money.

Now I knew the ropes, and I was determined to do better. I stayed at Bally's Casino Resort this time and again rented a car for convenience. After my six-hour flight, I checked into the hotel and then went down to the pool. I didn't care if it was 100 degrees outside. I dove into the pool, which felt like a bathtub, and let my body unwind.

This event was twice as expensive as the one from the previous year and attracted a lot more professionals. Poker celebrities such as Phil

Hellmuth, Mike Matusow, Annie Duke, and Todd Brunson (son of Doyle) were all participating. I would be competing against some of the best players in the world, but I was not intimidated. Everybody has a different destiny. I knew who I was. I was not a lesser human being because I was not famous or wildly successful or in possession of the material trappings of this world. It's who you are on the inside that counts, and our inner self is not always discernible to the untrained eye. These players might be big shots now, but their moment in the sun would fade away, and no one would even notice. Some, like Doyle Brunson, are icons who have earned lasting respect, but most are just flashes-in-the-pan who made a name for themselves within the confines of this small playground. With that perspective in mind, few people can hold power over you.

I paid my $3,000 entry fee and took my assigned seat. I was determined to bring my A game to the biggest tournament of my career. The director announced that we would play until only the final thirty-six players were left. In other words, it would be a fucking marathon! This could take up to sixteen hours of continuous play. Sure, there were breaks every couple of hours and then a one-hour dinner break, but it would still be a grueling event.

Hours went by, and I was holding my own—good decisions, no mistakes, and just enough luck to maintain a secure position. Players were now being steadily eliminated. I watched some of those big shots like Mike Matusow, Annie Duke, and Todd Brunson shuffling off into the sunset. I was still there.

Finally, it was time for our dinner break. I wandered through the Rio alone before landing at the sushi bar. It seemed like there were hookers everywhere. If you made eye contact even for a second, they'd seductively inquire, "You lookin' for a date, baby?" This was Sin City, and although some are intriguing to look at, I was there for one purpose—to cash a ticket in this tournament—so I tuned out all distractions and remained focused on the job at hand. When I returned from dinner, the director had combined tables to accommodate the remaining players. We had played for almost ten hours and there were about 100 players left of the original 400. The stakes were going up as we fought to the death to reach the final thirty-six.

Seated at my new table was one of the best players in the world, Daniel Negreanu. He appeared regularly in the big money games on TV. Some of those shows seemed like professional wrestling— good guys versus assholes fighting it out over huge cash pots. It was good entertainment, but unlike wrestling, it was not fake. This was for real money. Daniel was one of the good guys, and his nemesis, Phil Hellmuth, was one of the assholes. Probably, in fact, the biggest asshole. He had won more WSOP championships than anybody, yet he still acted like a fucking baby, insulting, whining, and crying. Maybe it was just an act, but not entirely. Nobody could act that poorly if they didn't already have it in them. Fortunately, Phil was at another table, but Daniel presented a different challenge. He was very friendly to everyone, very chatty—this was like a home game for him. He knew some of the other players at our table, but he didn't know me. He pointed to the healthy stack of chips in front of me and gave me the thumbs-up. He was a hard guy to dislike, which might have just been part of his charm offensive before he crushed you like a grape.

I was cruising along, biding my time, watching as more and more players were eliminated. I was playing conservatively, waiting for just the right moment to grab a big pot. I got involved in a hand with Daniel and allowed him to outplay me. It wasn't a big pot, but it bothered me because I knew better. Had I been more aggressive, he would've been forced to fold. Instead, I let him in the door, and he won the pot. There's an expression in poker, "Chicken today, feathers tomorrow." I had to cut myself some slack. I had been playing for almost twelve hours, and that was the first mistake I had made.

My next mistake would be much more critical. I still had plenty of chips in front of me to compete with, but one slipup could harm you irreparably. That came soon enough as I proceeded to play a hand that I had been folding all night. It was just good enough to get into trouble with. Did I play it in reaction to the hand I'd lost to Daniel? Maybe, since I believe that everything is connected as one thing quietly flows to the next.. The player I was up against was holding better cards and made me pay through the nose. My carelessness put a big dent in my previously respectable mountain of chips. I was wounded. How would I respond? I would have to reach deep down and release my secret powers.

My favorite card in the deck is the King of Spades. Most people are oblivious to the inherent symbolism in playing cards. In the Middle Ages, the four suits represented different strata of society. Hearts = the church, Spades = the military, Diamonds = the merchant class, and Clubs = the peasantry. The face cards all portrayed historical characters from the great civilizations, the Hebrews, the Holy Roman Empire, the Romans, and the Greeks. The King of Spades is the Biblical King David, the King of Hearts is Charlemagne, the King of Diamonds is Julius Caesar, and the King of Clubs is Alexander the Great. Queens and jacks also depict legendary characters, including Athena, the Greek goddess, and Sir Lancelot of

King Arthur's court. The most powerful card in the deck is the Ace of Spades, also known as the "death card." During the Vietnam War, thousands of these cards were dropped from the sky over peasant villages to instill fear in the enemy.

Card players are a superstitious lot who think they can simply will the appearance of a card through the power of their Third Eye. I myself have called on the King of Spades many a time to bail me out of a tight spot in a big pot. It does actually happen once in a while, and you remember those instances as being magical while forgetting all the times when applying mind over matter, whether in cards or life, has heartlessly let you down.

For me to continue onward, I would have to overcome this latest adversity. It was getting late, and the field was thinning out. My previous mountain of chips was now just a foothill, and I was holding on by a thread, my confidence shaken. This was the worst possible time to receive a frozen wave of cards. Soon I would be forced to play with mediocre hands that I had happily thrown away earlier. My chances of making it into the final thirty-six were running out.

The King of Spades is portrayed as a fierce warrior holding up the sword of Goliath, whom he famously slayed, and I tried to invoke the power of King David on my present battlefield but to no avail. I was eliminated in sixty-first place. After fourteen hours of play, mind over matter had eluded me, and I was crushed beneath the wheel.

The year before I had taken my defeat in stride, but this time was much worse because I had come so close. From the moment I lost that stupid hand to Daniel Negreanu, my trajectory had shifted downward. I don't like to be too superstitious, but I have observed that entire narratives often pivot on a single event. I have witnessed it happen in sporting events, where the final result can be traced back to a single play. In all things, there are turning points dictating good or bad outcomes. These are the laws of karma—cause and effect, action and reaction. What happened to me in the 2006 World Series of Poker was just a microcosm of cause and effect unfolding. I took it hard and felt crestfallen and alone.

I still had four more days to kill in the extreme summer heat of Las Vegas, and I tried to regroup, but I was what we would call "on tilt." This is a gambling term that means off balance, out of whack, and liable to blow a lot of money. And that I did. This was a rare state of being for me. I had always been a very centered individual. After fourteen hours of almost perfect play, I had come up empty in the biggest tournament of my life. Everything I had done, everywhere I had been, and every moment of my life had led up to this defeat. For three days afterward, I ate, drank, gambled recklessly, and blew ridiculous amounts of money in strip clubs. I entered higher-level poker games at the Bellagio and was predictably crushed by old timers just waiting for the overflow of defeated players drifting over from the Rio. When you're down and out in Las Vegas, there are no limits to the debauchery available right at your fingertips.

By the last day, I'd had enough. It was hot and crowded and noisy, and I couldn't wait to get out of there. I drove my rental car out to the serenity of Red Rock Canyon. To my dismay, I was greeted upon arrival by a big billboard—Toll Brothers at Red Rock, Luxury Condominiums Coming this Spring! *Man, they're even gonna fuck this place up*, I thought.

I walked down the scenic trails as the light reflected over the ancient rock structures. I looked up at the sun and breathed in the hot desert air, and I wandered down paths going deeper into the maze of red and brown stone. There are wild burros that still run loose in Red Rock Canyon. When you spot one, you feel as if you've been transported back to some prehistoric age. Driving out to this place was the smartest thing I had done in days. I was in the moment, and this was the psychic healing I needed. There in the desert, I remembered my name. Although my purpose in the universe has never really been clear, I've always been blessed with perseverance. In the fading light, I quietly reaffirmed the words of Heraclitis, "Character is destiny." These few hours in the stillness of Red Rock Canyon restored my peace of mind.

As the sun went down, I was no longer "on tilt." I slowly drove back into town, ate dinner at the hotel, and packed up for my flight home the next day. I never visited Las Vegas again.

CHAPTER TWENTY-THREE
COMMITMENT ISSUES

I T TOOK A WHILE FOR me to completely recover from the failure of my final appearance at the World Series of Poker. It was a setback, no doubt, but not a fatal one. I regained my footing at work and generated enough income to put the losses behind me. In the end, I simply chalked it up to experience.

I'd concluded long ago that several of my aspirations were not meant to be lifelong endeavors—songwriter, farmer, fisherman, carpenter, and even salesman—and now the latest addition to this dubious list, professional poker player. I had achieved a degree of excellence in each of those undertakings but not enough to go the distance in any one of them.

I continued to play in regular home games with my friends and in smaller tournaments in Atlantic

City, having always thought that poker, like golf, was an activity you could enjoy well into your old age. About ten years later, I realized that would not be the case for me. Financial setbacks would eventually put an end to that.

I did not hate my job, but I didn't love it either. I found the sales process stimulating but was turned off by the bullshit inherent in any office environment. All those personalities, opinions, and power plays colliding in the hallways added to an atmosphere of cynicism. Granted, I made a living in sales for years, but there were other things I preferred doing more. As mentioned before, I spent as much time as possible on the beach. I am unabashedly proud that I have continued this habit throughout my life. Some might say, "Oh, you can't make any money walking on the beach." They would be correct. However, the healthful benefits for my body, mind, and soul are undeniable. You just can't put a price on them.

I also continued to meet women either by chance or arrangement. My relatives often joked that I might have some commitment issues. They were being sarcastic, of course, but their assessment was spot on. I never even bought a house because I thought I wouldn't live long enough to pay it off. Longevity was not in my favor, particularly on my father's side of the family. My great-grandfather, Abraham, had died at sixty-six years old. My grandfather and namesake, Charles, had passed away at only forty-seven. My father had tragically died at fifty-nine years old. And yet somehow, I'm still here at seventy-three. In Jewish mysticism, the word *tzadik* refers to a righteous man. Only a *tzadik* shall be the last survivor of his family line. Rest assured that I am no *tzadik,* but I may well be the last of the Levinsohns.

I have often wondered how many of my ancestors perished during the Holocaust. My father's family was from the city of Vilna in Lithuania. Vilna was located on the far eastern border between Poland and Russia. It was the site of mass executions orchestrated by Nazi SS officers and assisted by the local anti-Semites. Many people know exactly how many of their family members were lost during the war. I do not. I don't recall it ever being discussed in our household when I was a kid.

I still visit the family cemetery once a year and place stones on the graves in keeping with the Jewish custom of remembrance. I see the spot where someday I will be buried and wonder if I am indeed the last survivor. When I stand before my grandfather's grave staring at the headstone with our shared name inscribed on it, I get an eerie feeling, as if I'm on the outside looking in at my own funeral.

For the time being, I am still here. The days run into each other and turn into years. There are so many things that fluctuate in life, such as people, places, money, and time. Memories fade as past experiences feel more and more like illusions, as if they never even happened. A few things remain the same, and although they are not tangible, they are often the most valuable. It's within the things that don't change that our true identity resides. That's what I hang on to. It's what keeps me traveling down an unknown road without signs or maps to guide me.

CHAPTER TWENTY-FOUR
THE DATE FROM HELL

EVEN IN MY FIFTIES, I was still getting fixed up on blind dates by optimistic wives of friends. I was intelligent, fairly good-looking, and I had some money, so I guess I was considered an eligible bachelor. Some of those dates went well, others not so well. I developed an approach to these awkward rituals—I would always just be a gentleman. That was easy enough to remember. Getting to know someone under these circumstances was a long shot, but it was still worth a try.

Being single for me could best be characterized as a steady conflict between freedom and loneliness. I needed my space but I craved intimacy and sex. I knew a lot of married couples, but I envied very few. I observed the boredom, the passive aggressive remarks, and the sense of resignation. Of course, that was offset by the stability, the genuine caring, and their clear vision of the future. Like everything else, it was a tradeoff.

I would be given a phone number, usually by my friend's wife, and my prospective date would be informed that I'd be calling. I'd turn on my most charming phone voice and arrangements would be made. These were almost always dinner dates. We'd choose a restaurant and take a drive, getting acquainted along the way. I'd hold the car door open, a simple gesture women appreciated, and. I always paid for these meals as was customary. Cocktails before dinner usually loosened things up. Some women exhibited affectionate tendencies right off the bat. Those early signals of encouragement could lead all the way to the Promised Land. Isn't that why we're in these awkward situations to begin with? We remember our young bodies pressed against each other as we slow danced on hot summer nights at the Colony, and while we may not be young anymore, we keep chasing that dream until the day we die.

When my friend's wife fixed me up on a blind date with a woman from her exercise class, I called her on the phone, and we immediately hit it off. We made a date for Saturday night. We were both excited. I showered, got dressed, and put on a modest amount of Paco Rabanne cologne. How could she possibly resist me? I drove to her house and rang the bell.

When she came to the door, I smiled and said, "Nice to meet you."

She said, "I'll get my bag."

Something seemed a little off. I held the car door open as always, and she got in. We drove to a beach bar for drinks and dinner. She was very quiet in the car. I tried to make conversation, but it was like pulling teeth. I asked her if she was okay, but she seemed to be having some kind of chemical meltdown.

Finally, she said, "I didn't like the way you looked at me when I answered the door, like you were disappointed in how I looked."

I said, "Not at all. You look great."

But she had already passed the point of no return.

We arrived at a bar overlooking the ocean and ordered drinks. I was trying to salvage the evening, but she looked miserable. Maybe she didn't like the way I looked. I suppose that was possible, as unlikely as that might be!

I said, "Listen, we're here. Let's make the best of it and have a bite to eat, and then I'll take you home."

She said, "I'm going to use the phone." She came back and said, "I called my ex-husband and asked him to pick me up, but he can't. I want to go."

We walked to the car, and I said, "I'm sorry you're so unhappy."

She rudely demanded, "Just take me home."

Finally having had enough, I replied, "I can't drive fast enough." I did not get the door for her this time.

We drove in silence and pulled up to her house.

She said, "Thanks for nothing."

I said, "No goodnight kiss?" No, I didn't really say that. I just thought, *Good riddance. What a psycho!*

I discovered the next day from my friend's wife that this woman was mentally unstable, and yet she'd fixed me up with her anyway! Never a fucking break.

CHAPTER TWENTY-FIVE
WELCOME TO THE COMPUTER AGE

I KNOW I ACT LIKE I never caught a break, but that's not really true. I'd heard Jack Nicholson say it once in a movie, and I just adopted it as kind of a goofy mantra. In fact, there were many times that fortune smiled on me in completely unexpected ways.

I was in my early fifties before I ever thought about getting a computer. They were available at work for sales proposals, but I felt no need to have one at home. Even though I wore a suit and tie to the office every day, I was still a blue-collar guy at heart, and technology was not a high priority for me. Then a friend of mine from our poker game told me his son had just graduated from college. They had bought him a new computer for graduation, and I could have his old one. It looked like a portable TV and weighed a ton. I got it set up and became familiar with some of its functions. He had not deleted anything on it, and I stumbled into an extensive file loaded with porn. He and his college buddies had downloaded tons of *Girls Gone Wild* videos and other even more explicit shit. I mean *much* more explicit. It went on and on. Maybe this was a research project for his senior thesis? I honestly didn't know how that kid ever graduated, but he did—magna cum laude!

Anyway, after perusing it several times strictly for educational reasons, I cleaned out the programs as best as I could. I remarked to my friend one night at our poker game, "You know, your son's a great kid, but he's got some serious mental problems! Do you have any idea what he's been doing all this time at college?" I told him about his son's hobby. My friend began beaming with pride. Apparently, as a young man, he too had been a psycho-sexual maniac. His boy was merely carrying on the family tradition.

Having a personal computer actually had a bigger impact on me than I'd anticipated. I had observed guys in Atlantic City listening to music on devices called iPods while they were playing poker. I thought, "I'd like to do that." I bought an iPod and purchased songs on my computer and then downloaded them onto the device. As a result, I have been enjoying the favorite songs of my life everywhere I go, including on the beach, on walks, and during poker games. I have valued the gift of music ever since Seymour Sussman took us to those shows at the Brooklyn Fox Theatre. And now, all these years later, my Apple iPod has enhanced my appreciation even more.

I also discovered the Word document application, which inspired me to start writing. I hadn't written much since the songwriting days of my late twenties but discovered that I had a lot to say on a range of topics. I completed my first essay at the ripe old age of fifty-seven. It was entitled "Time Waits for No One." I stole that title from a Rolling Stones song and got it published in a local newspaper. I soon became a prolific writer of essays on a variety of topics and submitted them to the *New York Times Magazine* and other major publications, but without success. I finally made a connection with a woman who was the editor of a small Brooklyn-based magazine. She published one essay of mine every month and even paid me fifty dollars per article. Technically, that made me a professional writer!

I built up a regular readership from among the people I knew. I'd send them my latest efforts, and their input became instrumental in my growth as a writer. Over time, I developed a distinctive style, which continues to evolve. It's philosophical and loaded with self-deprecating humor, the latter quality being what people seemed to like best.

I self-published an anthology of essays entitled *Levinsohn Abides* and a trilogy called *First Cousin of My First Cousin.* I expanded my efforts to include works of fiction, including a novella entitled *Regret* and a short story called *Ghost Town.* I relentlessly edited and re-edited every sentence and paragraph in search of perfection, and I continue like that to this day. And it all began because my friend gave me his son's old porn-laden college computer. That corrupted antique is now in a scrapyard somewhere, but the benefits from that unexpected gift continue to this day.

Ironically, Steve Pizza became one of my most valued reviewers. To be honest, I didn't even know he could read. He talked so fast and mispronounced so many words that you could barely understand him. The other guys broke his balls, but I would tell him, "You're smart, you're just uneducated." That happened to be true and was not intended as an insult, but he got mad whenever I said it. After finishing one of my stories, he always would say, "You missed your calling in life." To which I always replied, "Well, at least I'm writing now."

It's actually been fifteen years since I began writing seriously. During that time, my body of work has grown exponentially, as has my readership. The truth is had I started earlier, this might've become my actual career. A life as a writer would have suited me well, and I have often fantasized about such a life. In the end, it was just one more missed opportunity among many, although in this case I haven't given up yet. The real question is, "How far can I take it before I run out of time?" I guess that's a question that everyone faces at one time or another.

CHAPTER TWENTY-SIX
IMPENDING DOOM

ANOTHER SUMMER CAME AND WENT. And then suddenly, I found myself on the verge of turning sixty. It seemed like the days were flying by really fast, and there was nothing I could do about that. They say that happens more and more as you get older. Maybe it's because we know we're on the clock. You have a clock on you when you're younger too, but just don't know it.

I felt like I was in a dream, and my car was racing down a hill without any brakes. With only a steering wheel and fear to guide me, I deftly maneuvered through the oncoming traffic. Suddenly the road leveled off, and my car mercifully rolled to a stop. I woke up in a sweat and somehow was all right. That fucked-up dream pretty much sums up the aging process.

Ironically, what saved me from the added insult of accelerated aging was the same thing that held me back from material success—I don't rush. If you go at your own pace, there's a good chance that you're out of step with the rest of the world. If you wait long enough, the time comes when moving slowly pays dividends after all, just not in any financial sense.

And so now it was official. At sixty, I had outlived both my father and grandfather. I then set my sights on my great-grandfather, Abraham Levinsohn, who had arrived in America from Lithuania in 1893 and died at the age of sixty-six. Outlasting Abraham wasn't my only motivation in life, but it was some kind of weird benchmark. Having gotten this far, I felt like I was playing with house money, and every new day was gravy. That's a healthy outlook, although life can crush a thin perspective like that in a heartbeat. Many people I know can attest to that, but as it turned out for me, my sixties eventually became what I refer to now as *The Dark Ages.*

My illustrious position as a long-term care specialist was terminated by MetLife when they unceremoniously dropped long-term care insurance from their portfolio of products. The home office determined that my area of expertise was no longer profitable because people were actually using their policies. Their whole *raison d'être* was to sell products that people wouldn't use. In their perfect world, clients would just keep paying premiums while the company would keep depositing the proceeds into the general fund. All the while, this churning vat of revenue would be earning interest every second of every day. It's a brilliant business model that has been around for centuries, but this one time their actuarial tables were wrong, and they found themselves losing money. Interest rates were historically low at the same time that more and more people were going on claim. That's like a Category 4 hurricane for an insurance company. So, they just canceled the product and me along with it. Previously existing policies would be honored, but no new policies would be sold, effective immediately.

I stayed on for a while as a regular insurance agent, but I had invested too much time into mastering a specialty product that no longer existed. Other insurers followed suit, and there was a mad rush to the exits. Companies who previously promoted long-term care insurance as *"Necessary for the security and dignity of our seniors"* now changed their tune. The new corporate position became, *"Let's get the fuck out of here before these old bastards destroy us."* I started thinking that maybe their earlier compassion wasn't entirely sincere.

I still have my MetLife sales brochures depicting happy senior citizens meeting with an agent just like me, holding up their new policy that would protect them from financial ruin. A new generation of seniors would not be able to purchase this vital coverage. The corporations did not care. It was all bullshit.

I think back to the beginning of my career when I had lunch at a Chinese buffet with the veteran sales agent, who shared with me the benefit of his experience. His well-intentioned advice was, "Don't try to reinvent the wheel. Just trust management and follow their directions." Of course, shortly thereafter, he was terminated for not making his quota. Now it was only a matter of time before I would meet the same fate. The rug had been pulled out from under me the second they canceled my product. Avoiding humiliation, I turned in my letter of resignation before they could fire me.

I thought to myself, *What will I do now? I can't go back to construction. I'm too beat up for that line of work, and I'm certainly not moving back to Israel. That was a great experience when I was a young man, but it wouldn't be so great now.* It hit me that getting older was really complicating things. I had crossed the Great Divide—my past was now longer than my future. And with every day that goes by that equation gets worse.

I may have been down, but I wasn't out. If I had learned anything from the past, it was how to turn adversity into opportunity. I'd have to dip into that well once again, but the older you get, the harder it is to pull up the bucket. Fortunately for me, I still had some lifting power left.

As usual, the issue boiled down to money. This topic has plagued me my entire adult life, just as it had my father before me. I had some good years in both construction and insurance, but not in any consistent way, decade after decade. I have plenty of friends who locked onto one thing and stayed with it for their entire careers. As I was venturing into uncharted waters, they were busy accumulating. I've never been jealous of anybody in that regard— there's no payoff in that. Your bank account can provide financial security, but it can't guarantee long life, good health, or peace of mind. Those treasures are determined by mysterious forces far beyond our grasp. All that philosophical bullshit was great, but I still needed money to pay the bills. I didn't even qualify for unemployment benefits because insurance companies rigged the system to avoid contributing on behalf of their agents. We were designated as "statutory employees," which meant we were neither here nor there.

I tried to generate insurance sales working from home, but not everybody is cut out for that. I landed a few leads but nothing that would provide immediate relief. Out of desperation, I started driving to a casino outside Philadelphia to play cards a couple of times a week. I combined my poker skills with the Lyle Stuart method of quitting while you're ahead and managed to win fifteen times in a row; but I knew that level of success was not sustainable.

Then Big Tony called and said that a local limousine company was hiring. I tried to picture myself in that role and really couldn't see it, but I decided to check it out anyway. After two interviews, they ended up hiring me. They had an affluent clientele, and I had somehow made a good impression on the sales manager. I seemed intelligent, made a decent appearance, and could carry on a conversation. Just by checking those three boxes, any schmuck could probably succeed in a career in politics.

I had to go buy a black suit, while the limo company provided their standard yellow clip-on tie and a gold name plate for my lapel. I thought I looked like a douche bag, but I was willing to give it a try. The manager took me out on a couple of dry runs to Newark Airport, which was the primary destination for most of their clients. I quickly ascertained that this was not a high-paying gig. The veteran drivers would huddle together in the parking lot and complain about how much the company sucked. Low pay and long hours were their biggest gripes. There were also layers of management in place, resembling a paramilitary chain of command. This was not something I had responded well to in the past. Taken together, I was not optimistic about my chances for success in this latest endeavor.

Then the big day came when I was summoned to go on my first ride, a standard airport pickup. They had a big fleet of black Lincoln Town Cars and gave me the oldest, most rundown one on the lot. I wasn't sure it was even roadworthy.

I went down to meet my prospective passengers at the baggage claim. I held a placard with their name on it and stood there with the other drivers who were all holding up their signs. I looked around and saw that this was a motley crew of overweight, multinational, beat-up losers—in other words, my new fraternity brothers! I soon greeted my customers and carried their luggage to the car. I was witty and charming and got them home in one piece. I opened their doors and removed their bags from the trunk, feeling like an actor in a play. What the fuck! No tip? I called into the dispatcher, and he had no more rides for me. I returned the Lincoln, but as per their rules, I had to fill it up with gas and vacuum it. Fuckin' slave drivers. To make a long story short, I never went back. I then had to endure a lecture from Big Tony, who was born with a silver spoon in his mouth. I don't think he ever held a job that wasn't related to his family's construction business. He was a very well-meaning guy and a good friend, but he could never put himself in my shoes.

And lastly, those pants from that cheap suit I bought were so tight in the crotch that I couldn't stand it. There was no extra material to let out, so I tossed them into the dumpster. I still wear the jacket when I go to a funeral, so it wasn't a total loss.

Time went by, and I was virtually in no man's land. It's funny how quickly your savings can evaporate when you don't have a weekly paycheck. Playing cards several times a week wasn't cutting it. Even when you win, the cash never finds its way back into your checking account. It just sits in your drawer and is never used to help pay bills. I cashed in some stocks that I had bought when I was gainfully employed. But I tore through that and then resorted to borrowing money from my credit cards. It was interest-free initially but eventually switched over into a predatory lending situation. You have to be either a sucker or desperate to go down that road. I apparently was both.

I went on a few interviews with some local insurance companies. When I said that my area of expertise was long-term care insurance, they just kind of sighed. With nowhere to turn, I signed up with an internet job-search service. They emailed me potentially suitable opportunities and provided numbers to call to arrange a meeting. Unbeknownst to me, these sit-downs turned out to be group interviews. I'd sign in and grab a seat in a jam-packed room full of hopeful job seekers. There were probably a bunch of washed-out insurance agents among them. In some lost dream sequence, I might've seen the guy from the Chinese buffet sitting there. That would've been fitting.

Suddenly, like headliners in a Broadway play, a couple came striding up to the front of the room as speakers blasted the theme song from *Rocky*. These were the recruiters. Their opening was carefully choreographed with all the authenticity of Regis and Kathie Lee. Laughing at their own jokes and clapping their hands, they led with showstoppers like, "How's everybody doing today? You ready to make some money?" Then, changing gears, they tearfully paid homage to the late founder of the company, followed by their personal success stories. The guy mentioned that he'd just bought a new BMW but how it's not really about the money, it's about helping people. I looked around the room at the faces of the other attendees. They seemed mesmerized. It was like an evangelical revival. I personally was horrified by all this bullshit, but I still stayed until the end.

On my way out the door, I had to fill out a brief survey grading the presentation along with my contact info. In the name of expedience, I just answered five for every question, which meant highly satisfactory. That resulted in my getting a call the next day to come back for a personal interview. Out of sheer boredom, I went back and met with some guy who would determine if I had "the right stuff." He was twenty years younger than me and would be assigned as my mentor. Employing all the transparency of a bad car salesman, he attempted to sign me up right then and there. The whole thing struck me as a pyramid scheme and a waste of time, so I stumbled out of the door feeling like Willie Loman in *Death of a Salesman*.

CHAPTER TWENTY-SEVEN
DESPERATION ROW

I T IS ONE THING TO borrow money from a credit card company knowing you'll be paying exorbitant interest rates in the future. It's a whole other thing to attempt to borrow money from friends or relatives. I had spent decades working my ass off doing physical labor, followed by an extensive sales career in the insurance business. It felt pathetic to find myself in this situation, although fortunately I never fell into any deep depression about it. All my experiences had, over time, built up a resilient inner core that could get battered but not broken.

I meanwhile stumbled into several promising life insurance cases that might bail me out of my current dilemma. The most substantial one was for a young married couple whose wedding I had attended. I was friendly with the parents of the groom, who happened to be the guy who gave me the computer with all that porn on it. I naturally didn't mention that when I met with him and his young new bride. We sat at their kitchen table reviewing insurance plans and their associated costs. They asked excellent questions. I was thorough in my presentation and made them feel at ease. It seemed like a done deal. Now it would just be a waiting game while they decided which option to choose, and we planned to touch base again in a week.

A week turned into two. I was always low key in my approach to sales and many clients appreciated that as opposed to the high-pressure tactics they had come to expect. I waited to call the guy so as not to appear too eager. My funds were getting low and I needed this, but I couldn't let that influence my approach.

Meanwhile, I called my sister in Boston to ask her to lend me some money to help tide me over. That was something I had never done before. She asked how much I would need. I told her $5,000 and that I'd pay her back every month, starting immediately. I said that I had opened some promising cases but that these things take time. She said it was a lot of money, and she'd have to discuss it with her husband. I said I understood and appreciated it and that we'd talk soon.

I finally phoned the guy about the life insurance, and he told me that they hadn't decided yet and that he'd call me. I thought of that old line, "Don't call us, we'll call you." I was a little annoyed because I had done a lot of work on his behalf beyond just preparing the proposals. Confident that I would write this case, I diligently had sought out a carrier willing to insure him since he had a medical condition that was a deal-breaker for many companies. I succeeded in finding an insurer that would accept him and decided to call him with the good news. Maybe he was in a bad mood when I called, but he was a little rude to me. I considered mentioning this to his father but decided against it. Instead I closed the file on his case. I never heard from him again.

Meanwhile, I hadn't heard back from my sister either. I likewise waited a while to call her. When I finally reached her, I asked what happened when she spoke to my brother-in-law.

She said, "We can't lend you the five thousand dollars."

I asked, "How much are you able to do?"

"Actually, we can't give you anything."

I was silent for a few seconds. I had not been expecting that. We had always been very close, so this came as a bit of a blow. I didn't want to beg her, so all I said was, "No problem, I understand."

Shortly thereafter, I made my annual pilgrimage to the cemetery to place the commemorative rocks on the family headstones. It was an overcast autumn day, and there was no one else there. I slowly walked down the long driveway that was lined with tall sycamore trees. I was feeling kind of melancholy as the wind picked up and blew through the leaves on the trees. In Hebrew, the word *ruach* means both wind and spirit. I was feeling the spirit in the air as I approached our ancestral plots. At this point in my life, the only family I had left was my sister and her family. I looked up at the majestic sycamores swaying in the breeze and suddenly felt a deep sadness at her refusal to help me. That feeling stayed with me for a while but eventually dissipated. I loved my sister, so I put it behind me. We've never spoken of it again.

Everybody has been disappointed by others, it's just a part of life. I accept that. Everybody has a different journey. I tend to walk through the world slowly and alone. Some people are born with a silver spoon and others with a jagged fork, but neither is determinative of one's ultimate fate. The expression, "Character is destiny," becomes clearer as one's story unfolds. The seeds are sown early, but the harvest arrives late.

I was now sixty-four years old and struggling but determined not to take early Social Security benefits. I understood the pitfalls of that desperation play, knowing that I'd basically be locking in a lower amount for the rest of my life. I had to hang on for another two years before I would reach full retirement age. It's ironic that all everybody wants is to stay young, and then suddenly you're wishing you'd get older sooner. That's an unnatural state of affairs. Only money could cause that.

Meanwhile, I sat down in the poker casino one day and waited for my name to be called to enter a game. There were some guys sitting there I didn't know, and I could hear their conversation. One guy said, "I'm telling you, this Uber gig is the best thing that has happened to me in years. I can drive for them and still play cards here whenever I want. I love it." I had heard of Uber but didn't really know what it was, so I asked him about it. He explained what was involved and how to get started. If I used the code he gave me when I signed up, he would get a bonus. I initially applied online using his code and then drove up north for a personal interview. They did a background check on me and before I knew it, I was an Uber driver!

I still needed money until my new job started generating income, so I decided to ask Steve Pizza for a loan. The guys at our weekly poker game liked to joke about how much cash Steve had hidden in his attic. After all, he did operate a successful pizzeria for forty years, and that was a cash business. I asked him straight out if he could lend me $5,000, and to my amazement, he said yes without hesitation. I met him that night at a local restaurant, and he handed me an envelope with fifty $100 bills in it. I was floored that he would do this. I told him that I would pay him back an agreed upon amount every month and asked him how much interest he wanted. He said none. My preconceived notion that every Italian in New Jersey was a natural-born loan shark was proven wrong. It took a while, but I paid him back every cent. I will never forget that it was Steve Pizza who helped me out in my time of need.

CHAPTER TWENTY-EIGHT

HAVING STRUCK OUT AT MY one day of employment for the limousine company, I was now learning the ropes as a newly commissioned Uber driver. At least now I didn't have a bunch of bosses overseeing my every move. As an independent thinker, I am not cut out for that kind of supervision. Now I was just a driver. "I go right, I go left, I go straight..." I reveled in the simplicity of that.

Once I'd mastered the rudimentary tasks of the Uber app on my iPhone, I could respond to ride requests, pick up passengers, and take them to their destination. Sometimes it was near, sometimes it was far. The majority of riders were nice, with the exception of the occasional asshole. I took the good with the bad and went with the flow. I started whenever I wanted and finished whenever

I wanted. That guy in the poker room was right when he said that driving for Uber was a good gig.

What I was not expecting was such a deep dive into the vagaries of the human condition. With so many people getting in and out of my car, I was now exposed to a full spectrum of personalities. Business commuters, day laborers, foreign tourists, and drunken college girls all entered my space for short periods of time. I became the ultimate host.

I never anticipated that I would end up doing this every day for the next five years. Half a decade disappeared in the blink of an eye. During that time, I had more than 5,000 riders in my car. In my lifelong quest for excellence, I managed to maintain a top driver rating according to Uber's performance metrics. Even more astonishing was that not one person ever threw up in my car. Given that a major component of Uber's business model was chauffeuring around drunken idiots, I considered this to be one of my greatest achievements in life. Granted, I had some close calls and had to pull over on the side of the road more than once to let some nitwit puke his brains out. I eventually refused to pick up party revelers after St. Patrick's Day festivities. The mere thought of the vast quantities of green beer consumed by unruly college girls superseded the earning potential of that holiday.

You can't make a lot of money as an Uber driver unless you're willing to beat the shit out of your car by driving thirty or forty thousand miles a year. I was pretty extreme during my first two years on the job while trying to keep my head above water and also pay back Steve Pizza. When I reached full retirement age at sixty-six, I started receiving Social Security benefits, which allowed me to taper back my Uber driving. First thing I eliminated was those insane pickups from the late-night bar scene. I needed money, but I didn't have the tolerance to have drunken lunatics hanging out of my windows, shouting obscenities. One time, I glanced over and saw a passenger snorting cocaine on the seat next to me. I told him to put that shit away. Fucked up young people tend to test the patience of middle-aged drivers. That's when you ask yourself, is this really worth it?

I remember passing through Asbury Park on a summer night and seeing all the partygoers staggering around on the streets and sidewalks. Sometimes it seemed like all of America is drunk on firewater. An idea struck me for a sequel to Martin Scorsese's *Taxi Driver*—Robert De Niro reprising his role as Travis Bickle but now as a semiretired *Uber Driver*. I had to pitch this to Scorsese! My enthusiasm for this project would be contagious—"It's gold, Marty. I tell you it's gold!"

One of my earliest rides was picking up five teenage girls in the affluent town of Spring Lake. They piled into my car and immediately asked me to connect their music to my car speakers. I was still new at this and very accommodating. They started blasting the latest Taylor Swift album and singing at the top of their lungs.

Hunched over the wheel, I'm thinking to myself, *What the fuck am I doing?* I tried to imagine a sixty-five-year-old Robert De Niro playing the part of me. In my script, he politely asks the girls to turn the volume down and when they ignore him, he pulls a gun out of the glove compartment. "I'm putting on Sinatra now, and if you don't like it, get the fuck out!" One brave soul starts to complain, and De Niro turns to her and says, "Are you talkin' to me?" That's the money line! "It's gold, Marty. I tell you it's gold!"

Back on Earth, those entitled brats were only going three miles. I made eight dollars with no tip. After that, I stopped being so accommodating.

Uber is a good source of supplemental income if you have other money coming in. I was still receiving some monthly insurance renewals, which, along with my newly acquired Social Security benefits, eased the pressure on me. Nevertheless, I would never be financially secure as it was painfully obvious that I had made a ton of mistakes to end up like this.

I thought to myself, *Once I was young and carefree, but now I am old and on Social Security and Medicare.* I don't understand how this happened. This is the great mystery of life, and the whole human race is galvanized by this same nagging question.

I was even forced to quit playing poker because grinding out a living as an Uber driver made a losing streak at cards untenable. My friends couldn't believe that I would quit, but I did, and I never looked back. They would ask, "But don't you miss it?" And I would answer, "Sure, I'll play again someday, but just not now." As time went by, I realized I would probably never play poker again.

On the plus side, this job gave me the freedom to relax on the beach between my self-imposed shifts. As always, I went there when there weren't many people around. The one thing that still disturbs me most is the littering. I have witnessed little enclaves of people who are clearly not locals sitting in circles, enjoying our natural habitat. Then they pack up their stuff to go home, leaving behind a mess of beer cans, submarine sandwich wrappers, and empty bags of chips. What a bunch of fucking assholes! This particular beach is not maintained by our town other than to provide garbage cans near the stairs. Hence, I refer to it as a self-cleaning beach because any debris left behind is simply washed away by the high tide. The beautiful ocean becomes an invisible garbage dump, that is until the next tide washes the intruders' shit back in. I have thought about going to pick up the refuse of these oblivious fools, but in all honesty, I don't want to touch it. I have also thought about approaching these interlopers, whom I assume drove down from some godforsaken place like Staten Island, but I don't. When I see their over-sized muscles and head-to-toe tattoos, I don't want any confrontations. And those are just the women! The guys have arms bigger than my legs, so I just sit there watching these Neanderthals through my peripheral vision while my opinion of the human species sinks like an untethered boulder drifting unimpeded to the ocean floor.

One day I took a break from driving and stopped for a bite to eat at Max's, which is an iconic Jersey Shore restaurant known for its hot dogs and char-broiled burgers. I sat at the counter and ordered a hot dog and a root beer and impulsively ordered cheese fries, something I'd never ordered before. I was trying to convince myself that I liked them when three people entered and sat down right next to me. It was the middle of the afternoon, and the entire place was empty. Why did they have to sit right on top of me? It was a young woman with a little kid and an older guy. The owner came over and told them children are not allowed at the counter, something about insurance liability. They moved to a table in the back.

I was studying those cheese fries when the young woman walked past me on her way to the ladies' room. She stopped right in front of me and dramatically flipped her hair back and tied it in a ponytail. For some reason, I commented on her dexterity. She approached me and said that she really wanted to sit next to me, but they wouldn't let her. I wondered, *Why would she want to sit next to me?* She volunteered that it was her birthday and that she was twenty-three. I asked if the child was her son. He was. I asked if the man was her father. He was not, but rather just a friend who drove them. She was wearing a low-cut top and tight shorts, looked Spanish, and was very pretty and very friendly. Suddenly she offered me her phone number. Being a little slow on the uptake, I asked her what she did for a living. She moved closer and quietly said that she was in adult entertainment. "Now I see," said the blind man. I asked in what capacity, and she said she would tell me when we were in a more intimate setting, and I should definitely call her. Then she returned to her table.

I didn't give it much thought except that it was odd for something like this to happen in a family restaurant like Max's. The next day, I drove up the coast looking for Uber customers. I was parked in a commuter lot outside the ferry terminal to New York when suddenly I saw the young woman with her kid and the older guy walking right by me on their way to the boat. It was surreal seeing them out of context in this faraway place, like a dream sequence. I was so stunned that I didn't even speak up and say hello. That night while out driving, I impulsively called her to say that I had seen them at the terminal. She replied that her son wanted to go on a boat ride and then she wanted to know when I wanted to get together. I was ambivalent about that possibility. I had no girlfriend at the time and it was tempting, but it also seemed dangerous at many levels. I wondered if I might be out of my mind for even entertaining this idea.

For the record, I never did pursue that scenario with her. After all, I was old enough to be her grandfather! She did text me one day and asked if I would meet her for lunch at Max's. Was I unconventional enough to become friends with a twenty-three-year-old Puerto Rican hooker? Why not? Her name was Elena. We candidly discussed her business model, services rendered, rates, and so on. I found her to be an intelligent young woman stuck in a lucrative but scary lifestyle. I felt sorry for her but avoided the instinct to advise her. Even though she was pressing her smooth, shapely leg against me the whole time, I fought off the temptation of becoming her newest customer. I may have been adventurous, but I was no daredevil. Elena had taken a cab to the restaurant, so I gave her a ride back to this fleabag hotel in Belmar where she was staying. I couldn't really fathom the nature of the life she was leading. Time went by, and I didn't hear from her.

The Jewish holidays came that year, and as is the tradition, I fasted on Yom Kippur to atone for my many sins. I spent the day being more reflective than usual, and at sundown, I ate some chicken soup to break the fast. The holiday was over, so I thought I would go drive Uber for a while. Why not? As I drove down Ocean Avenue and into Sea Bright, I quickly got a ride request from a local bar. Some guy climbed into the back seat and instantly fell asleep even though his destination was only ten minutes away.

I got to his place and said, "Hey, buddy, wake up. You're home."

He stumbled out of the car and handed me a ten-dollar tip and then went into his apartment building. As I drove away, I heard a shuffling of papers in the back seat. I pulled over and spotted some money on the seat. At first I thought it was just a few singles, but upon further inspection, I saw it was a roll of bills—three hundred dollars to be exact! I guess in his inebriated state, his bankroll never made it back into his pocket. *Wow, this must be my lucky night!* I mean, I couldn't call him since his number got deleted by the Uber system when I dropped him off. I didn't know his last name, and I didn't know which apartment he lived in. This had to be a gift from the universe for all those times I'd been ripped off.

Who was I kidding? I couldn't keep this money, and not because I'd just atoned for my sins on Yom Kippur. I'm too honest in general. Why else would I be driving Uber at this stage of my life? So I contacted the company, they contacted the guy, he called me, and I returned his money the next evening. He was so grateful that he gave me a fifty-dollar reward just for not being a thief.

Then out of the blue, Elena sent me a text asking if I could lend her forty dollars. It seemed odd that she would ask me of all people, but I drove to Belmar and gave her the fifty dollars that had just been given to me. There were no strings attached. I was just paying it forward. It is not often that I do a good deed, but it felt rewarding to help someone whom I barely knew. I never heard from Elena again.

Little episodes like this make you think about all the people who have come and gone in your life, no matter how briefly. I remember driving an elderly couple I picked up at Newark Airport. They were returning from a vacation in the Bahamas. They were old and frail, but they were sporting nice suntans. They could barely walk, but they were dressed in bright and fashionable clothes. I loaded their suitcases into the trunk and helped them into the back seat. As I attempted to merge onto the New Jersey Turnpike, there was an inordinate amount of rush hour traffic. I carefully zigged and zagged and maneuvered through the maze of vehicles into a clear, flowing lane. I heard the old man speak his first words since we left the airport, "Good job, driver." I smiled to myself. *He called me driver!* That brief acknowledgment of achievement would have to suffice for a lifetime of mixed reviews. The voice of the universe had spoken, and I had been redeemed, at least for the moment. *Thanks for those kind words, old timer.* Of course, he didn't tip me after I dropped them off, but his little compliment was a better gratuity than money.

Many passengers seemed to take an inordinate interest in the business model of Uber. It captured their imagination, and I became a conduit to fill in the blanks of their curiosity. "How long have you been doing this? Do you like it? Can you make a living at it?" If they opened that particular door, I would reply, "This would be a good job if everybody tipped us the same way they tip cab drivers." Sometimes that discussion resulted in a gratuity, sometimes not.

I was surprised at how much I was transformed by the sheer volume of human contact in personal transportation. I used to be a quiet and introspective type. I wouldn't say that I was sullen, but I certainly wasn't overly interested in anybody's life story. I now found myself drawing people out in discussing their careers, their families, and, in some cases, their darkest secrets. I wasn't exactly a priest, but as an anonymous driver, their confessions were safe with me.

My study of the human condition led to discussions with characters from every walk of life, with the possible exception of the homeless, who by definition have nowhere to go. If someone's head was buried in their cellphone, I would not disturb them. I particularly enjoyed engaging with affluent passengers regarding their careers. Most people like to talk about what they do, especially if they are asked intelligent questions. I was a good listener and had refined my ability to raise the level of inquiry beyond just the mundane. I injected philosophy and humor where appropriate, which stimulated the conversation even further. These captains of industry were surprised to discover that their lowly Uber driver was, in fact, a Renaissance Man.

It then struck me that it was my own human condition I should be examining. I was a perfect case study of success and failure. I represented all that is good and bad, weak and strong, caring and indifferent. I was the ultimate mixed bag, and the people I transported were branded by the same flames of imperfection as my own shaky resume. We may have been separated by wide gaps in position and status, but we had more in common than met the eye. Everyone has problems—they're just different problems. For some reason, I find comfort in that realization.

CHAPTER TWENTY-NINE

THE END OF THE LINE

WHEN THE PANDEMIC OVERWHELMED THE nation in the beginning of 2020, everything stopped. Here on the Jersey Shore, all nonessential businesses closed. New York City shut down and became a ghost town as the flow of commuters and tourists came crashing to a halt. The malls were empty, there was an eight o'clock curfew on the roads, and restaurants could only offer takeout food and deliveries. Even the beaches and board-walks were off limits to pedestrians just wanting to get a little fresh air. The roads were empty, and the whole atmosphere was eerie and dead quiet. I was on the verge of turning seventy in the midst of an apocalypse.

My final Uber ride was on March 15, 2020. I received a call from a woman to pick up her friend who needed to go to a medical emergency clinic.

The rider was an Asian woman who did not speak English. She wore a mask and was clearly ill. I thought to myself, *Oh, no, does she have Covid?* All that was known at that time was that the virus had come from Asia. She was coughing and in obvious distress. I opened the windows and drove as fast as I could to the medical office about thirty minutes away. Worried for myself and for her, and hoping she could understand me, I kept looking back at her and saying, "Hold on, hold on. We're almost there." I really thought she might die in the back of my car. I finally got her to that office and then called her friend. I chastised her and told her that woman needed an ambulance, not an Uber. She added a tip to the fare but that was not the point.

After that, there was no longer a reason to continue driving. There were no riders and no destinations. Everybody was just staying home and waiting. The only ones in need of transportation were drug addicts going to methadone clinics. My Uber days had come to a screeching halt as the world settled into a new reality based on fear and uncertainty.

There was a steady head count shown on TV of new cases, new hospitalizations, and new deaths, every day, day after day. It felt like the End Times that doomsday prophets preached about on obscure Sunday religious broadcasts. Six feet of separation was the new world order. This was only three years ago by the time I'm writing this, but it seems like another lifetime now.

I remember going into a supermarket and finding that the shelves were virtually bare. No toilet paper, no paper towels, no bottled water, no nothing. There was panic buying and hoarding. I was lucky to find two boxes of whole wheat linguine sitting alone in the pasta section with a couple of jars of Ragu sauce. We had become a nation of survivalists.

Everybody was self-quarantining. Since I was essentially living a solitary life anyway, I joked with my friends that I had been preparing for this for years. I started writing every morning and taking two-mile walks every afternoon. That is basically what I still do now.

Needless to say, my social life fell off dramatically during the pandemic. In fact, I'd rarely dated after becoming an Uber driver. Any hopes of romance were placed on the back burner. I was not ashamed of my new job. I just worked every weekend because that was the prime time for earning. I was in my mid-sixties when I became an Uber driver and had become accustomed to a daily routine of writing, walking, and driving. Still, it was not a bad existence. I was free, peaceful, and healthy, and I didn't answer to anyone. Not everyone can say that.

CHAPTER THIRTY

NOSTALGIA

TIME GOES BY AND ONE thing leads to another. As the decades roll by, the lines separating experiences get blurry, and we lose focus of the big picture. That is probably my motivation for writing this saga, to better understand the connective tissue behind the seemingly unrelated episodes of my life. It is starting to finally come together as memories rise to the surface, adding color and detail to the canvas.

My seventieth birthday came and went with a deeper than usual period of self-reflection. "Seventy" has this funny ring to it that you can't quite wrap your head around. It just *sounds* old. We have been conditioned from the time we were kids to think like that. In fact, we probably even associated old age with thirty years old. I guess when you are only twelve that would make sense.

I have devoted a lot of thought to how I got from Point A to Point B. Half a century had blown by in the wink of an eye, and I could not just abide the disappearance of those fifty years bracketed by careless youth and impending old age. Everyone I know is walking around in a daze and wondering, *Where the fuck did the time go?* Reawakening my powers of deductive reasoning, I managed to solve the big mystery! Every morning upon waking up, I swing my legs out of bed and watch my feet hit the floor. This has happened over and over again, one day at a time, year after year. By my calculation, it's happened in my life more than 20,000 times. Bingo! I was young and now I'm old! A whole lifetime had slipped away in steady and silent increments while I was too distracted to even notice. That may be a simplistic analysis for an issue that has plagued mankind for centuries, but the explanation somehow provides me with a sliver of hope. Who knows, maybe I'll watch my feet hit the floor another 5,000 times.

Meanwhile, these big benchmark birthdays tend to spark deep contemplation of past experiences and future expectations. If I could just slide down the rabbit hole of memory without the chains of judgment, then I could revisit my glory days with greater clarity.

Music is always a good vehicle for time travel. When I was about ten years old, my father took me to Niesen's Music Store in Asbury Park to buy a guitar. We settled on a Gretsch acoustic guitar, which I still have to this day. That purchase led me to take guitar lessons from one Mr. Andre Taloff. I don't know how my parents found him, but he would come to our house once a week after school to teach me how to play. He was an old man from Italy with white hair who would show up with his guitar case and some instructional books. I actually can remember the name of one of those books, *Mel Bay's Guitar Course for the Beginner.*

I learned how to read music and play basic notes and chords. I wonder now how much my father paid Mr. Taloff back in 1960. I remember that he smelled like an old man (whatever that means), even though he was probably twenty years younger than I am now! He was a little impatient with me, maybe because I didn't exactly want to be there. I thought it would be cool to play the guitar, but I wanted to be outside riding my bike or playing with the neighborhood gang. One time, those kids came up onto our lawn and saw me through the window taking my lesson. They were making faces at me and mocking me because I was a prisoner in my own house.

I labored through my afternoons with Mr. Taloff. He once played for me "Malaguena," which was a Spanish song made famous by the guitar virtuoso Andre Segovia. I was impressed by his complex technique of flamenco strumming. He showed me how to play those chords, and I got it. Then I thought, *Fuck those kids! I'm learning something I can take with me for the rest of my life while they're riding around in circles on their bicycles!* And sure enough, five years later, I was standing on the stage at the Colony Surf Club with The Voltaires, playing lead guitar on "Sleepwalk!" Thank you, Mr. Taloff.

Music provided the background for the early amorous encounters of our preteen years. It started in about sixth or seventh grade with the infamous make-out parties. These hastily arranged get-togethers would spring up when somebody's parents would be out for the evening. Boys and girls would show up at a classmate's house and congregate in a dark wood-paneled den. The room would be graced by several couches, some snacks on a table, and the key furnishing, a record player. Upon arrival, the girls automatically gathered together, chatting while the boys proceeded to act like idiots. After things settled down, the real business at hand would commence. The host would dim the lights and put on a Johnny Mathis album. It is ironic that kids so consumed by trying to be cool would be drawn to a square like Johnny Mathis singing "Strangers in Paradise." The reason was simple—every song was a slow dance. Partners quickly found each other in an instinctive ritual not unlike the way penguins find their mating partners. We swayed to the music while our young bodies were suddenly pressed against each other. Some couples then retreated to the couches to engage in the delights of French kissing.

This went on for several hours until the dreaded time approached when the parents would be returning home. I can't speak about what kids do nowadays, but nobody was getting pregnant at these early parties. That level of sexual maturity would arrive soon enough during high school.

With every passing year, our connection to music got stronger and stronger. The soundtrack of the '60s would be marked by a collision of influences wearing out record players of crazed teenagers everywhere. There was the British Invasion, featuring the Beatles and the Rolling Stones. When the Beatles appeared on *The Ed Sullivan Show*, the entire country tuned in and lost its mind. Musical variety shows inundated network TV lineups. *American Bandstand*, *Hullabaloo*, and *Shindig* showcased popular rock groups. Black artists appeared on *Soul Train*, which featured the incredible sounds of Motown as the studio audience rocked out on the dance floor. Record sales soared. The combined influence of the British Invasion, American rock, and Motown swept over the country like a tidal wave.

And standing at the top of the mountain was Bob Dylan, whose songwriting and scratchy voice would be an inspiration for every kid with a guitar.

To this day, when the organ introduction to "Like a Rolling Stone" kicks in, the entire universe still begins nodding its head as one.

Instead of make-out parties, we now had high school dances every weekend. At the Jersey Shore, these events were presided over by the local legend, Louis "Buzzy" Lubinsky. Buzzy grew up in Bradley Beach and was the son of Herman Lubinsky, the owner of Savoy Records in Newark. Herman had a reputation for being exceedingly cheap in business, yet he supplied his son with an expansive collection of 45-rpm records. Buzzy, who was a trained drummer, would set up two turntables with his drums in the middle on a small stage in the back of the dance hall. As his advanced sound system blasted out songs in perfect sequence, Buzzy played his drums along with every hit record he spun. This was early performance art. With his Beatle haircut and impeccable taste in music, Buzzy Lubinsky was the most coveted DJ on the Jersey Shore. Sadly, this musical icon died as a virtually forgotten man at the age of sixty.

In high school, there were several social fraternities. The Barnstormers wore flashy jackets and only accepted the most popular kids and athletes of Italian and Irish heritage. They may have all been Catholics, but they weren't exactly pious. Then there were the Ravens, who had a similar membership, but were a little rougher around the edges. There was a fraternity just for Greeks, and then there were the Jesters, who only accepted sociopaths and future criminals. And lastly, there was a fraternity exclusively for Jews—Upsilon Lambda Phi, or more commonly known as Ulps. It was kind of like Hollywood Country Club, except for kids! In my senior year, I was elected to be treasurer. It was not really as exalted a position as it may sound.

Every summer, the Barnstormers took a weekend canoe trip down the Delaware Water Gap. This was a dangerous undertaking that required a lot of planning. It was somewhat arrogant for a bunch of teenagers from a beach town to try and navigate the whitewater rapids of the Delaware River. The brother of one of my closest friends was the president of the Barnstormers. Terry Weldon, despite being left back in grammar school, possessed undeniable leadership qualities. In fact, he went on to become the popular mayor of our town. Unfortunately, he got indicted for bribery and was sent to prison. Afterward, he got sick and died. I went to his wake. He may have been a felon and an ex-con, but he remained a beloved guy to those who knew him. The line to get into the funeral home went around the block.

I only bring this up because my connection to Terry caused me to be invited on the big canoe trip down the Delaware River. I wasn't a member of the Barnstormers, and I was the only Jew in history to ever be invited. What a glorious honor! I shared a canoe with Terry's younger brother. His given name was James, but everybody called him Doots. To this day, I still don't know the origin of that nickname. On the last day, Doots and I smashed into a boulder, our canoe capsized, and all our shit floated downstream. In that moment, I learned that trying to be cool was sometimes overrated.

Without question, the biggest event in this period of our lives would be getting our driver's license. Our whole world changed in a flash as freedom from our parents' tight leash was now within our grasp. Our raging hormones could have room to find expression in the privacy of the back seats of our own cars. The world of teenage dating had arrived with a bang.

Now we walked through the halls of the high school, eyeing up potential girls to ask to the movies on a Saturday night. The now-defunct Eatontown Drive-In Theatre was a popular destination for date night. Then it was on to Stewart's Drive-In for pizza burgers, followed hopefully by a ride out to one of the quiet spots deemed appropriate for "parking." This was the main event. If you were lucky, you might be out with a girl experienced in the art of French kissing. Some girls were well developed by now, and if your date liked you, she might even let you feel her up. The next step was dry humping in the backseat. This was an awkward exercise in simulated fucking. Those backseats were narrow, and despite our fumbling around, we eventually found a way to get our bodies lined up just right. I'm not embarrassed to admit that kissing and grinding in the back seat of a car at seventeen would lead to some of the greatest orgasms in human history.

A couple of years before I turned seventy, I started receiving emails regarding my fiftieth high school reunion. I admittedly had little interest in this event. I found the thought of reuniting with my former classmates somewhat depressing. I only knew them as young and hopeful teenagers, not as washed out, middle-aged retirees. Since I am in total denial regarding my own aging process, an extravaganza like this could shoot holes in my entire strategy. The women I lusted after as nubile teens are now grandmothers of college students. Soon they'll be great-grandmothers! I don't need that.

To be clear, I was not and am currently not a misanthrope (at least not most of the time). There were many high school classmates of whom I had fond memories. I simply didn't consider a fiftieth anniversary of anything to be a cause for celebration. On the contrary, I considered it a cause for mourning and the gnashing of teeth. It was just another reminder that we were young, and now we're old. I'm glad most of us have survived—the morbid list of our departed classmates notwithstanding. But let's face it, our best days were behind us and five or six hours of cocktails, appetizers, and fleeting nostalgia would not change that. I tried to picture my presence at this event, and it didn't go well. I imagined everyone limping through the doors with a mixture of trepidation and anticipation. As people squinted to read the nametags on everyone's lapels, they'd howl with the joy of recognition while concealing the horror at the generally decrepit appearance of their former classmates. The men I admired and the women I desired would be shadows of their former selves. And after one or two people asked what I had been doing for the last fifty years, I would've run for the hills.

As you might have guessed, I did not attend the gala festivities. I heard afterward that it was a blast, and in retrospect, I was wrong and should've gone. I would've probably enjoyed traveling down memory lane with some old friends. Nostalgia can be a great tonic for the soul, and I do believe humor and pathos are our saving graces. If you can just laugh at yourself for some of the stupid shit you've done in your life, then you might be saving a lot of money that would otherwise be spent on psychotherapy.

When I think back to those innocent times, there is one song that has stayed with me throughout my entire life. It is not a rock song, and it is not a soul song. Written by Jimmy Webb and performed by Richard Harris, "MacArthur Park" was a seven-minute operatic tribute to the passion of young romance. This was an unlikely song to be at the top of anybody's list of all-time favorites. The lyrics were incomprehensible, and the musical arrangement was pretentious. It featured an instrumental break that was as long as the rest of the song. Recklessly changing tempo and key, it built to a dramatic crescendo without regard for the limited attention span of the listening audience. I am amazed they even played it on the radio, given that the average pop song was only three minutes long. The humor columnist Dave Barry once conducted a poll that decreed "MacArthur Park" was the worst song ever written. I didn't care what he said, and the test of time has proven him wrong.

Fifty years later, I might be walking on the beach listening to my iPod when the piano introduction to "MacArthur Park" comes on. Something clicks in my brain as Richard Harris begins to sing. As a classically trained actor, he'd played King Arthur in the movie *Camelot* and now inhabited the leading role of this song with that same commitment.

I tried to imagine Jimmy Webb sitting at a piano, struggling with the complex elements of "MacArthur Park." I envisioned the moment of inspiration when his monstrous experiment, like *Frankenstein*, suddenly took on a life of its own. Jimmy Webb surrendered to forces greater than himself and became a mere vessel through which this creation was formed. I don't really know if it happened like that, but I like to think that it did. "MacArthur Park" takes me back to the most hopeful time in my life, when everything was in front of me.

I am now seventy-three. I have had many lovers over these many decades, yet never married. As time has passed, excessive idealism and a fear of commitment combined to forge my destiny. Every woman has contributed to the twin peaks of my emotional history—a mountain of love and a mountain of pain. They're all part of the same primordial experience, every one unique and special, yet all melting into a single romantic extravaganza. Looking back, I realize there wasn't anything better than young romance. It's the one pure break we catch in this life. In a perfect world, we could just hold onto that feeling of being young and in love and never let go. But it's an imperfect world, and we quietly grow old against our will.

Musical memories are so powerful that an entire industry has been built around the nostalgia of "Oldies" concerts. Ironically, the executive producer for the Oldies revivals on PBS is TJ Lubinsky, the nephew of Buzzy Lubinsky! For some reason, he never credits his uncle as a source of inspiration for his success. I'll bet that TJ even inherited Buzzy's massive record collection, but I guess the late legend was probably the black sheep of the family. I just wish TJ would have the decency to invoke Buzzy's name at least one time.

These productions remind me a lot of the old Murray the K shows from the Brooklyn Fox Theatre. It's one great act after another, with the obvious difference being that all the performers are now significantly older and a lot less nimble. These former teen idols, having fought the aging process with every ounce of a lifetime of narcissistic celebrity, reprise for the 10,000th time their greatest hits. The wildly applauding audience, comprised of my own contemporaries, is bopping, albeit out of rhythm, to the sounds of what in retrospect were the best days of our lives.

I attended a reunion party a couple of years ago of a band that included my friend Jeff, who was the former drummer of The Voltaires. The group was called The Society, and they were among the next generation of bands to emerge after The Voltaires. They lasted for several years and carved out a place for themselves in the crowded sea of Jersey Shore beach bands. Now they were all approaching seventy and wanted to revisit their glory days. I stood in the back of the small but boisterous audience as the band stumbled through some of their old hits. They were rusty and hadn't played together in decades. The inebriated crowd was happily bopping to familiar, yet shaky renditions of Paul Revere's "Kicks," the Beatles' "I Saw her Standing There," and Wilson Pickett's "The Midnight Hour." The keyboard player, who hosted the affair, had been practicing basically every day since childhood. This was more than a casual hobby to him, and he seemed disappointed that his aging bandmates couldn't keep up with him. He opened the closing number with a rousing organ solo from The Rascal's "Good Lovin'," but halfway through the song he abruptly stopped playing. The timing was screwed up, and he was pissed off. The jam session was over! I half expected him to shout into the microphone, "Now everybody get the fuck out of my house!"

As a writer always seeking inspiration, an event like this offered a treasure trove of material regarding something near and dear to my heart. It connected a lifelong love of music with my obsession regarding the passage of time. I wrote a scathing but humorous review entitled "The Reunion" and was shocked that it didn't get picked up by *Rolling Stone* magazine. Of course, that would have required me to submit it—an important part of the process! My premise was that The Society's reunion bash was evidence that efforts to relive the past are often well-intentioned but not easily executed. Just look at the legion of dreamers throughout history who sought the elusive fountain of youth. Those cockeyed optimists rejected any notion that their calling was just a pipedream and a waste of time.

Of course, they're all dead now, but at least they went down swinging. And despite my best efforts, someday I too will be joining them on the other side.

CHAPTER THIRTY-ONE
NOSTALGIA PART TWO

T HE POWER OF NOSTALGIA IS not limited to music only—we likewise cherish memories of TV shows, movies, sporting events, and primarily our own personal anecdotes. Some people dismiss the concept of "living in the past" as a waste of time, but the past occupies a much greater percentage of our lives than the present and future combined. And that breakdown only increases with each passing day.

As a young boy, I sometimes accompanied my father to his clothing store in Asbury Park. In that era of safety, a kid could freely roam around the downtown area of Asbury. For reasons still unbeknownst to me, I got in the habit of shoplifting those old 45 rpm records from a variety store on Cookman Avenue. I had built up quite a collection and was fearless in my technique. It was pretty basic. I would feign interest, look around, and if no one was looking, I would stick some records under my jacket and casually walk out of the store. On one particular raid, I stole several records, including one that my mother liked, "What Kind of Fool Am I?" by Anthony Newley. As I left the premises with my stolen goods in tow, a voice called out to me, "Hey, Skip, what do you have under your jacket?" It was the store detective and I, a ten-year-old, had been busted! He asked who I was and then marched me down to my father's store. I cried out, "But I took it for mother!" Those words fell on deaf ears. I sat in shame in the storage room among the boxes of shoes, scared to death and whimpering like a rain-soaked dog. My father came in and had mercy on me. He patted me on the head and told me to take it easy. Driving home that night, he asked what I thought my punishment should be. Not being overly hard on myself, I suggested that I not be allowed to buy any records for a month. He said he wouldn't tell my mother because it would kill her.

About a week later at our Friday night dinner at my grandmother's house, my mother, out of the blue, commented to no one in particular that stealing is a terrible thing. I didn't have to be a genius to realize that my father had ratted me out. I looked right at him, and he couldn't meet my eyes. Feeling betrayed, I could barely finish my matzo ball soup that night.

Growing up as I did, Jewish kids did not do physical labor beyond parking cars at beach clubs. I guess I was the exception to that tradition when I began working summers for our maid's boyfriend, Willie Warrick. Why we even had a live-in maid is a question without an answer. We lived well, but we were not rich. I think we just pretended to be.

Willie was a talented house painter and wallpaper hanger. He had an amiable personality, and through word of mouth had built up a good reputation among the residents of Deal. He was an alcoholic, but that did not interfere with the quality of his work. He maintained a crew that he picked up every morning and drove to the job. Willie taught me how to scrape old paint off wood trim, use a roller, and eventually cut in edges with a brush. At the end of the day, I had to shake out and fold the drop cloths, clean the brushes with Varsol, and store the leftover paint. I would have hated this job if Willie hadn't been such a nice guy. His crew didn't pay too much attention to me, but they were all right. They managed to show up for work every day despite getting totally inebriated the night before. My most vivid memory is of sitting in the middle of the van between Willie and Johnny with Nick sleeping in the back seat. I can recall the acrid smell of stale beer, turpentine, and body odor. A skinny fifteen-year-old Jewish kid riding in a beat-up van with three hungover, middle-aged Black guys on our way to work. That snapshot in time represents a real-life education that was not available in school.

With that training under my belt, I undertook some painting jobs while I was still in college. Through word of mouth, a local dentist hired me to paint the woodwork in his house. He had a beautiful home, a beautiful wife, and beautiful children. Among other things, he asked me to paint the trim inside his walk-in closet. I had always considered myself to be smart, but on that day, I experienced a serious lapse in judgment. I attempted to paint his clothes closet without actually removing the clothes! I accidentally got white paint on the sleeve of his leather sports coat. It was purple and soft and looked very expensive. Apparently, he had bought it while on holiday in Italy. Without thinking, I compounded my original poor decision with an equally boneheaded second one. I wet a rag with turpentine and attempted to remove the white paint from the sleeve. What I removed was the purple pigmentation! I looked in horror at the destruction I had wrought on this once-fabulous garment. Who knew that it was his favorite? Now comes error number three: I turned the jacket around on the closet pole so the good side was facing out, I cleaned up my stuff, and quickly left.

In life, there are probably about a half a dozen phone calls that you wish you never got. That night was one of them. My explanation was ludicrous, my apology insufficient. And since I could not compensate him with a new purple jacket from Italy, I simply never returned to face him or collect my pay. My career as a painter had unceremoniously come to an end.

Sometime thereafter, I ended up playing in a tennis group that included the very same dentist. No mention was ever made of the beautiful leather jacket I had destroyed. He was a nice guy. I was shocked to learn years later that he'd committed suicide. God only knows why he did it. He seemed to have had everything you could ever want. His was just one life out of millions, and everybody has to die sometime, but that news really shook me up.

The river of nostalgia is deep and wide and runs the gamut from the ridiculous to the sublime. I could go on indefinitely with more tales of personal fiascos. My list of fuckups is like a menu in a Greek diner. If I reached down deep enough, I might find noble deeds hidden in that resume of disasters, but it's the misadventures that define us as imperfect people in an imperfect world. Nobody's hands are clean from regrettable errors in judgment. Fortunately, most of our transgressions are forgiven, even if not entirely forgotten. I not only remember mine but have memorialized them in these pages. It helps me maintain a sense of humor about myself, without which I would be a zombie. The lost episodes of our lives are like valuable artifacts buried in the fields of distraction. It's good to dig them up sometimes and let them bask in the sunlight.

CHAPTER THIRTY-TWO

LEVINSOHN'S LAST SUMMER

B ACK IN THE GLORIOUS '70s, I became a prolific reader. I tore through the novels of preeminent American authors, such as Hemingway, Fitzgerald, and Steinbeck. In that era of upheaval, it was also trendy to read the assorted works of a German-Swiss writer, Hermann Hesse. *Steppenwolf, Siddartha, Beneath the Wheel,* and *Demian* were among his more notable titles. Buried in his extensive bibliography was a novella written in 1919, *Klingsor's Last Summer.* This was the tale of a famous German painter living out the final days of his life in southern Switzerland. He had one last burst of creativity before slipping into a state of extreme mood swings, alternating between exuberance and dread. I inserted my own name into that title and used it repeatedly with several of my friends just as a joke. Every year, I would muse that this summer would be my last.

Several years ago, I was sitting on the beach in the late afternoon when suddenly the sky turned dark and ominous. I ignored the first droplets of rain and intermittent flashes of thunder and lightning, thinking they would pass. When the sky fully opened up, I grabbed my stuff and headed for home, which was a mile away. Struggling through sheets of driving rain and harrowing winds, I feared that my aluminum chair would serve as a lethal conduit, and I would be struck dead by lightning. I thought my literary prophecy was coming to pass right then and there. Fortunately, I made it home in one piece. Since then, when storm clouds have arisen, I have been a little faster in heading for the exits.

Having weathered that particular storm, along with countless others in different arenas, I continued to come and go as I pleased. I may have been untethered to social conventions, but I sensed that my freedom was an illusion. That was a recurring theme in the work of my hero, Bob Dylan. The imagery running through his lyrics implies that nothing is as it seems, and everything comes with a price. I have tried to imagine Dylan's process as he composed those songs. The words seemed to have flowed through him as if he were not even there, as if he were in another dimension. This applies to artists from every discipline, including athletes, who likewise entered a zone where they just couldn't miss. Pure artistic inspiration has probably been the redemption of the human race, given all the fucked up shit people have done to each other throughout history. This might explain our addiction to the escapism present in all forms of entertainment. Music, movies, sports—we cling to these diversions like lifeboats in a raging sea. Without them, we might go under.

Spring is almost here again, and I can picture myself walking on the beach in the very near future. Maybe the legend of Levinsohn's Last Summer will endure for yet another season. I have spent my whole life taking it one step at a time. That's a lesson you learn when you're a walking man.

CHAPTER THIRTY-THREE

DUST IN THE WIND

I HAVE NOT REALLY HAD MANY mentors in my life. Of course, I loved my parents and my grandparents, but they were not mentors as I did not follow in any of their footsteps. I had teachers and contemporaries who taught me things, but I generally tended to go my own way.

There was one friend of my father, Eddie Lichtig, who was a successful entrepreneur in the field of construction. Not that he ever did any work himself. In fact, I doubt if he ever picked up a tool in his life. What he did was form a company that concentrated on home renovations, often to lower middle-class homeowners. He then created a finance company to lend his customers the money to pay for the job. Finally, he bought a lumberyard to provide construction materials for his workers, as well as the public at large. It was a brilliant circular business model. I always thought he was the sharpest guy among my parents' friends. Not wanting to overexert himself, Eddie would arrive at his office late in the morning and then stop by the various jobsites. Every afternoon in the summer, he would head to the Breakwater Beach Club, where he would take a swim in the pool and then relax on a chaise lounge. He inevitably fell asleep, despite the fact that his wife and her friends were chattering away right next to him. He made a fortune, spoiled his children, took a lot of vacations, and was the master of his own destiny.

When my father was dying from ALS, I moved back to New Jersey from Kentucky to help out. Eddie gave me a job as a carpenter's helper on one of his crews. That is where I first learned to swing a hammer and operate a power saw. That experience propelled me to eventually becoming a master carpenter. Ten years later, I started my own company, DuroCraft Construction. Who better to seek guidance from than Eddie? He told me to meet him at his beach club one day after work. I arrived early and patiently waited until he finished his nap. He then devoted his full attention to me, discussing specific recommendations for my ambitious new undertaking. Of course, I eventually went bankrupt, but that was not due to any advice given to me by him. I managed that all on my own.

My father sadly passed away at the early age of fifty-nine. Some years later, I heard that Eddie was also not well. One day I was eating lunch with a friend at a local deli when I spotted Eddie and Dr. Alvin Weinstein sitting at a table across the room. The good doctor, who was affectionately known as "Ubbie," was a longtime friend of our family. He and his wife even visited me when I was living in Israel. He was the one who broke the news to me regarding the gravity of my father's illness.

Ubbie had been a doctor and captain in the army during World War II. He was among the American forces that liberated Dachau concentration camp. What he saw at Dachau was unimaginable to me. I don't know if those images get permanently seared into someone's brain. Maybe they can be washed away over time. I wish I could ask him now. I only know that Ubbie was a good man who always had light in his eyes despite the darkness that had surrounded him upon entering hell on Earth.

I glanced over at them and saw Ubbie reaching across the table and feeding Eddie a spoonful of chopped liver. Tears welled up in my eyes. Eddie had dementia. I got up and walked over and shook hands with Ubbie. I was always glad to see him. I then knelt down and put my arm around Eddie's shoulder and looked into his face and smiled. I saw some little flicker of recognition in his eyes.

I wanted to believe that he knew me. It broke my heart to see the sharpest guy I'd ever known come to this. Nothing makes sense.

Phillip Roth wrote, "Old age isn't a battle, it's a massacre." A couple of years ago, a masonry crew came to my apartment complex to replace all the sidewalks and steps. It was a big job, and they were working there for several months. For some reason, the entire crew all had long hair and beards, which was unusual in this day and age. That is what I looked like when I did that work down in Kentucky, and I still look like that now, my gray beard notwithstanding. I briefly entertained the thought of asking the owner for a job as a laborer. It was kind of a half-baked idea since I was then pushing seventy with a bad back. I mentioned this to Big Tony, who, in no uncertain terms, discouraged me from pursuing this harebrained scheme. He was right. I was just reaching backward in my ongoing denial of getting old.

I usually walk about two miles every day. I have been taking scenic walks along the ocean, in the woods, and on country roads for the past fifty years. When I was younger, I walked closer to four miles, but two miles is good enough for now. I currently have several routes near the shoreline that I prefer. As I drift along on my chosen path, I listen to the favorite songs of my life on my iPod. This winning combination has served me well for many years.

I am impervious to the weather as I adapt my clothing to the ever-changing conditions. For some reason, I have developed a reputation as an extremely slow walker—that is according to several people who occasionally have accompanied me. They affectionately mock me for this idiosyncrasy. I take their remarks in the spirit they are given. But I know a secret—the slower I go, the longer I last. Rushing has always been antithetical to my nature. To the untrained eye, this might be perceived as a character flaw, but in reality, it has been a hidden blessing.

I am ambivalent about what age I would like to live to be. Given my family history, I never expected to make it this far. At seventy-three, I possess a mental road map of where I fell down and where I rose up again. My memory may be imperfect, but it's close enough. I can recall almost every place, every job, every woman, and every friend. I regret how much time I wasted, but I'm not alone in that regard. All my victories and defeats are just illusions to me now, despite the importance I placed on them at the time. If I learned nothing else from my career as a poker player, it was the transient nature of hands won and hands lost. My obsessive recordkeeping of those outcomes was merely an exercise in vanity. That historical transcript is now as brittle as the papyrus buried beneath the pyramids. It will never be found, and it will never be read.

EPILOGUE

Every night I lie in bed and stare at the slivers of light drifting in through the shade. I breathe in and I breathe out—that's how I know I'm still here. I am a solitary man, which has its benefits and deficits. I don't have to do anything or go anywhere unless I want to. And I answer to no one. All that freedom comes with a price. I consequently lack real connection, extended family, or sense of community. I consider it a fair tradeoff.

I am grateful for what I have received and not embittered by what I have not. My self-portrait has now been filled in with the colors of experience. Can I persevere until one day I become a righteous man, a true *tzadik*? Then, as it is written, I could rest knowing that I was indeed the *Last of the Levinsohns*, although it is doubtful that will be inscribed on my headstone.

I tend to operate on the premise that everything is connected. I assume that every action has a reaction, which in turn generates additional reactions, creating never ending ripples of consequences waiting quietly behind the scenes. Everybody has wondered what might be different had they taken another turn at a critical fork in the road. But time machines only exist in Hollywood screenplays and in the fantasy world of daydream believers. There's no payoff in obsessing about what might have awaited us down some unknown road. In moderation, regret is melancholy and strangely peaceful. In its extreme, it can be destructive.

I could have stayed on the path laid out for me by my well-intentioned parents. I would have sailed through school as the excellent student that I always was without missing a beat. I might have graduated from law school with honors and went on to a stellar career as a high-profile attorney, or possibly even a judge like my grandfather. I would've had a loving marriage, beautiful children, grandchildren, and lived on a country estate. Prestige, wealth, and status would have been the hallmarks of the life I did not choose.

I have struggled with this missed opportunity my whole life. Poor judgment has eclipsed the landscape of my aspirations at many a turn. Occasional bouts of bad luck are built into the human condition, and I have had my share just like everyone else.

But then I wake up as if from a dream and find myself as I am today, walking on the beach...breathing in the salty air...at one with the universe, if only for a moment.

With the passing of time, I have gained perspective on the things that I have done and places I have been. I have outlasted my cynical old mantra, "Never a break, never a break." Instead, I embrace the ancient adage, "Character is destiny." All things work together, and I've come to accept the twists and turns of the roller-coaster ride of my life. I'm no mountain climber, but it's been a rocky ascent just to reach this plateau of peace.

It is impossible to comprehend the consequences of the seemingly random turns on the lost highway. Everybody has made mistakes, everyone has regrets, and everyone has wondered what if I did this instead of that. But as I drift along through the fading light, I realize that my whole life has led up to this moment...right here...right now. This is all there is and all there will ever be. Everything else is simply washed away in the sands of time, a veritable illusion stashed in the hidden archives of some future reckoning.

THE END

ACKNOWLEDGMENTS

I want to thank CL2 for her invaluable input, as well as my old friends MSS, RPA, JS, DP, JV, and many others for their longstanding support.

I also wish to acknowledge the great work of Debra and her team at The Pro Book Editor, who elevated my efforts through their experience and professionalism.

ABOUT THE AUTHOR

Charles Levinsohn is a writer, music lover, and beach walker. He was formerly a fisherman in Israel, a farmer in Kentucky, a carpenter, a salesman, and a poker player. As a rambler and a gambler, he recognized the fleeting nature of wins and losses. His fascination with the relentless passing of time is a recurring theme throughout his work.

Some of his literary efforts include an anthology of essays entitled *Levinsohn Abides*, a short story called *Ghost Town*, a novella entitled *Regret*, and a trilogy called *The First Cousin of My First Cousin*. He lives in Monmouth Beach, New Jersey.

Visit the author's website at:
charleslevinsohn.com

Connect with the author on social media at:
https://www.facebook.com/charles.levinsohn
https://twitter.com/CharlesLevinso6